Church of Scotland, Church Service Society

Euchologion - a Book of Common Order

Being forms of worship issued by the Church Service Society. Fourth Edition

Church of Scotland, Church Service Society

Euchologion - a Book of Common Order
Being forms of worship issued by the Church Service Society. Fourth Edition

ISBN/EAN: 9783337291495

Printed in Europe, USA, Canada, Australia, Japan

Cover: Foto ©Lupo / pixelio.de

More available books at **www.hansebooks.com**

Ευχολογιον

A

Book of Common Order:

BEING

FORMS OF WORSHIP,

ISSUED BY

𝔈𝔥𝔢 𝔈𝔥𝔲𝔯𝔠𝔥 𝔖𝔢𝔯𝔳𝔦𝔠𝔢 𝔖𝔬𝔠𝔦𝔢𝔱𝔶.

FOURTH EDITION, CAREFULLY REVISED.

WILLIAM BLACKWOOD AND SONS,
EDINBURGH AND LONDON.
MDCCCLXXVII.

Prefatory Note.

IN issuing the fourth edition of their Book of Common Order, the Church Service Society desire to acknowledge, with gratitude, the large success that has hitherto attended their labours; and to express the hope that their fathers and brethren, in the ministry, and the congregations of the Church may find this volume aid their devotions, and promote the order and solemnity of their worship of Him, who must be worshipped in spirit and in truth.

Contents.

	PAGE
PREFATORY NOTE,	vii
TABLE OF PSALMS AND LESSONS FOR DIVINE SERVICE ON EVERY LORD'S DAY THROUGHOUT THE YEAR,	5
" OF SELECTED PORTIONS OF THE PSALMS, PARAPHRASES, AND HYMNS,	17
" OF PSALMS AND LESSONS FOR SPECIAL SERVICES,	21
" OF DAILY LESSONS,	29
" OF PSALMS FOR EVERY MONTH,	43
THE ORDER OF DIVINE SERVICE—	
FIRST SUNDAY OF THE MONTH,	47
SECOND " " "	69
THIRD " " "	90
FOURTH " " "	110
FIFTH " " "	131
" " FOR THE ADMINISTRATION OF HOLY BAPTISM TO INFANTS,	150
" " FOR THE ADMISSION OF CATECHUMENS TO THE CONFIRMATION OF THE BAPTISMAL VOW, AND TO THE PARTICIPATION OF THE LORD'S SUPPER,	159

THE ORDER FOR THE BAPTISM OF ADULTS, . .	165
" " FOR THE CELEBRATION OF THE LORD'S SUPPER, OR HOLY COMMUNION, . .	173
" " FOR THE SOLEMNIZATION OF MATRIMONY,	190
" " OF DIVINE SERVICE AT THE BURIAL OF THE DEAD, ...	199
" " OF SERVICE AT THE ORDINATION OF MINISTERS, ...	220

APPENDIX—

I. CONFESSIONS, ...	233
II. SUPPLICATIONS, ...	236
III. THANKSGIVINGS, ...	239
IV. PRAYERS FOR ILLUMINATION, ...	243
V. ASCRIPTIONS OF PRAISE, ...	244
VI. INTERCESSIONS, ...	247
VII. THANKSGIVINGS FOR SPECIAL OCCASIONS, .	255
VIII. INTERCESSIONS FOR SPECIAL OCCASIONS, . .	260
IX. COLLECTS AND PRAYERS FOR SPECIAL OCCASIONS, ...	271
X. BENEDICTIONS, ...	302
XI. EXHORTATION, WHICH MAY BE USED AT THE HOLY COMMUNION, ...	304

Table

of

Psalms and Lessons

FOR DIVINE SERVICE ON EVERY LORD'S DAY
THROUGHOUT THE YEAR;

AND OF

PSALMS AND LESSONS FOR SPECIAL SERVICES

TOGETHER WITH

A TABLE OF DAILY LESSONS

AND A

TABLE OF PSALMS FOR EVERY MONTH

Table of Lessons, &c.

THE Lessons for Morning and Evening Service on the Lord's Day form a two-years' course. The First Lesson in the Morning Service is selected from the historical books of the Old Testament, on the principle of conveying an outline of the sacred history; and the First Lesson in the Evening Service is taken from the prophetical writings, the order of the canon being followed throughout. The Second Lesson combines portions of the gospels and epistles. It will be observed that the greater part of the New Testament is thus read yearly on the Lord's Day—the gospel history being harmonised so as to admit of being completed within the year; while the portions, whether of gospels or epistles, necessarily omitted one year, are introduced, so far as possible, in the year following.

In the "Table of Lessons for a Third Service," the First Lesson is chosen principally with reference to the Sunday Morning Old Testament Lesson, and the Second Lesson is taken from the gospels in their canonical order.

The Table for the First Year is to be used in those years of which the number is odd, as 1877-79, &c.; the Table for the Second Year in those of which the number is even, as 1878-80, &c.

When Psalms and Lessons are specified in the "Table of Lessons, &c., for Special Services," as proper for a special occasion, the Psalms and Lessons of ordinary course are then to be omitted.

It is intended, when several Psalms are set down, that a selection should be made at the discretion of the Minister.

According to the "Table of Daily Lessons," the Old Testament is read through once, (with the exception of certain parts omitted as less suitable), and the New Testament twice, every year.

When a Psalm or Lesson is described as extending "*to*" a verse, it is to be understood that the verse specified is excluded.

Table
of
Psalms and Lessons
for
Divine Service
on
Every Lord's Day throughout the Year

TABLE OF PSALMS AND LESSONS FOR DIVINE SERVICE ON EVERY LORD'S DAY THROUGHOUT THE YEAR.

FIRST YEAR.

Morning.

Lord's Day of the Year.	Month and Day.	Psalms.	Old Testament Lesson.	Gospel.	Epistle.*
1	Jan. 1, 2, 3, 4, 5, 6, 7	1, 2	Gen. 1 to 2, v. 4	Luke 1 to v. 26	Acts 1
2	„ 8 Jan. 14	5, 6	„ 2, v. 4	„ 1, v. 39 to v. 67	„ 2, v. 22
3	„ 15 „ 21	9	„ 3	Matt. 1, v. 18	„ 4, v. 32, to 5, v. 17
4	„ 22 „ 28	12, 13	„ 4	Luke 2, v. 21 to v. 40	„ 6
5	„ 29 Feb. 4	16, 17	„ 6, v. 9, to 7, v. 11	„ 2, v. 40	„ 9
6	Feb. 5 „ 11	18, v. 30, 19	„ 7, v. 11, to 8, v. 13	Matt. 3	„ 10, v. 24
7	„ 12 „ 18	22	„ 8, v. 13, to 9, v. 20	John 1, v. 19 to v. 35	„ 12
8	„ 19 „ 25	25	„ 11 to v. 10 and v. 27, to 12, v. 11	„ 2	„ 15, v. 40, and 16
9	„ 26 Mar. 3	28, 29	„ 13	„ 3, v. 22	„ 19 to v. 23
10	Mar. 4 „ 10	32, 33	„ 14 to 15, v. 7	„ 4, v. 43	„ 21, v. 17 to v. 37
11	„ 11 „ 17	35	„ 17 to v. 23	Mark 1, v. 16	„ 22, v. 30, to 23, v. 11
12	„ 18 „ 24	37	„ 18, v. 16, or 19, v. 12 to v. 30	John 5 to v. 19	„ 26
13	„ 25 „ 31	39, 40	„ 21 to v. 9, and 22	Mark 2, v. 23, to 3, v. 20	Rom. 1 to v. 18
14	April 1 „ 7	42, 43	„ 24 to v. 29	Matt. 5, v. 27	„ 3, v. 19, to 4, v. 9
15	„ 8 „ 14	45	„ 24, v. 29	„ 7	„ 7, v. 21, to 8, v. 18
16	„ 15 „ 21	47, 48	„ 27 to v. 41	Luke 7, v. 36	„ 11 to v. 22
17	„ 22 „ 28	50	„ 27, v. 41, and 28	Matt. 13 to v. 24	„ 13
18	„ 29 May 5	52, 53	„ 32	„ 8, v. 18	„ 14, v. 19, to 15, v. 14
19	May 6 „ 12	56, 57	„ 37	„ 10 to v. 24	1 Cor. 1 to v. 26
20	„ 13 „ 19	60, 61	„ 41, v. 14	Mark 6, v. 20 to v. 47	„ 4
21	„ 20 „ 26	64, 65	„ 42 or 43	John 6, v. 41, to 7, v. 2	„ 12 to v. 28
22	„ 27 June 2	68	„ 45 to 46, v. 8	Mark 7, v. 24	1 Cor. 14 to v. 20
23	June 3 „ 9	70, 71	„ 47, v. 27, and 48	Matt. 16, v. 13	„ 15, v. 35

PSALMS AND LESSONS.

#	Morning	Evening	Psalms	First Lesson	Second Lesson	
24	June 10	June 16	73		Matt. 18 to 19, v. 2	2 Cor. 3, v. 12, to 4, v. 7
25	— 17	— 23	75, 76		Luke 10 to v. 17	" 5, v. 11, to 6, v. 11
26	— 24	— 30	78 to v. 32		John 7, v. 32, to 8, v. 2	" 11, v. 16, to 12, v. 14
27	July 1	July 7	79	Gen. 49	" 8, v. 31	Gal. 3
28	— 8	— 14	82, 83	Ex. 2	" 9, v. 39, to 10, v. 22	" 6
29	— 15	— 21	86	" 3 to 4, v. 19	Luke 11 to v. 29	Eph. 4 to v. 25
30	— 22	— 28	89	" 7 or 9 or 10	" 12 to v. 32	" 5, v. 22, to 6 v. 10
31	— 29	Aug. 4	91, 92	" 12 to v. 43	" 13 to v. 10	Philip. 1 to v. 27
32	Aug. 5	— 11	95, 96	" 13, v. 17, and 14	John 11 to v. 46	Col. 1, v. 9, to 2, v. 6
33	— 12	— 18	99, 100, 101	" 16	Luke 14	1 Thess. 4, v. 13, to 5, v. 12, or ch. 5
34	— 19	— 25	103	" 17	" 16	1 Tim. 1
35	— 26	Sept. 1	105	" 19 to v. 14, and 20 to v. 22	" 17, v. 20	2 " 2
36	Sept. 2	— 8	107	" 24, v. 4, to 25, v. 23	Mark 10, v. 2 to v. 31	Titus 2 to 3, v. 8
37	— 9	— 15	110, 111	" 26, v. 30, and 27 or 28 to v. 22, and v. 29 to v. 42	Luke 19, v. 2 to v. 29	Heb. 1 to 2, v. 5
38	— 16	— 22	114, 115	" 30 to 31, v. 12	John 12, v. 20	" 9
39	— 23	— 29	118	" 32	Matt. 21, v. 33, to 22, v. 15	" 12
40	— 30	Oct. 6	119, v. 17 to v. 41	" 33 or 34	Luke 20, to v. 20	James 3
41	Oct. 7	— 13	119, v. 57 to 81	" 35 or 40	Matt. 25 to v. 31	1 Peter 2, v. 11, to 3, v. 13
42	— 14	— 20	119, v. 97 to v. 121	Levit. 6, v. 8	" 26 to v. 20	2 " 1
43	— 21	— 27	119, v. 137 to v. 161	" 7, v. 7	John 13, v. 21	1 John 1 to 2, v. 3
44	— 28	Nov. 3	120, 121, 122	" 10	" 14	3 John
45	Nov. 4	— 10	126, 127	" 23 or 25, to v. 24	" 15, v. 18, to 16, v. 5	4
46	— 11	— 17	130, 131	Num. 13, v. 17, to 14, v. 26	" 17	Rev. 1
47	— 18	— 24	134, 135	" 16 to v. 36	Matt. 26, v. 57	" 2, v. 18
48	— 25	Dec. 1	137	" 16, v. 36, and 17 to 18, v. 8	John 18, v. 28, to v. 39	" 4
49	Dec. 2	— 8	139	" 21	" 19 to v. 25	" 6
50	— 9	— 15	141, 142	" 22 to v. 36	" 19, v. 25	" 14
51	— 16	— 22	145	" 22, v. 36, and 23	Luke 24, v. 13 to v. 36	" 17
52	— 23	— 29	147	Deut. 4 to v. 32, or 4, v. 44, and 5	John 20, v. 19 to 31	" 19
53	— 30	— 31	90, 91	" 6 or 29, and 30, v. 15	" 21, v. 15	" 21

* When it is necessary to shorten the service, one of the New Testament Lessons may be omitted.

TABLE OF PSALMS AND LESSONS FOR DIVINE SERVICE ON EVERY LORD'S DAY THROUGHOUT THE YEAR.

FIRST YEAR.

Evening.

Lord's Day of the Year.	Month and Day.	Psalms.	Old Testament Lesson.	Gospel.	Epistle.
1	Jan. 1, 2, 3, 4, 5, 6, 7	3, 4	Prov. 1, v. 20, to 2. v. 10	Luke 1, v. 26 to v. 39	Acts 2 to v. 22
2	— 8 Jan. 14	7, 8	" 8	" 1, v. 57	" 3
3	— 15 — 21	10, 11	Eccl. 1, v. 12, to 2, v. 18	Matt. 2 to v. 21	" 5, v. 17
4	— 22 — 28	14, 15	" 11, v. 7, and 12	Matt. 3	" 8 to or from v. 26
5	— 29 Feb. 4	18 to v. 30	Isa. 1 to v. 21	John 1 to v. 19	" 10 to v. 24
6	Feb. 5 — 11	20, 21	" 2	Matt. 4 to v. 12	" 11
7	— 12 — 18	23, 24	" 5	John 1, v. 35	" 13 to v. 14
8	— 19 — 25	26, 27	" 6	" 3 to v. 22	" 17, v. 16
9	— 26 Mar. 3	30, 31	" 8, v. 11, to 9, v. 8	" 4, v. 4 to v. 43	" 20, v. 17
10	Mar 4 — 10	34	" 11 and 12	Luke 4, v. 16 to v. 33	" 21, v. 37, to 22, v. 30
11	— 11 — 17	36	" 13 to v. 14	Mark 2 to v. 14	" 25
12	— 18 — 24	38	" 14	John 5, v. 19	" 28, v. 16
13	— 25 — 31	41	" 22	Matt. 5 to v. 27	Rom. 2
14	April 1 April 7	44	" 24 or 25	" 6	" 5
15	— 8 — 14	46	" 28	Luke 7, v. 11 to v. 36	" 8, v. 18
16	— 15 — 21	49	" 29	Matt. 12, v. 22 to v. 50	" 12
17	— 22 — 28	51	" 32 or 33	" 13, v. 24 to v. 53	" 14 to v. 19
18	— 29 May 5	54, 55	" 35	" 9, v. 10 to v. 34	" 15, v. 14
19	May 6 — 12	58, 59	" 41	" 10, v. 24	1 Cor. 1, v. 26, and 2
20	— 13 — 19	62, 63	" 42	John 6, v. 22 to v. 41	" 10, v. 13, to 11, v. 2
21	— 20 — 26	66, 67	" 44	Mark 7 to v. 24	" 12, v. 28, and 13

PSALMS AND LESSONS.

22	May 27	June 2	..	69	Isa. 45 to v. 14	Mark 8 to v. 27	1 Cor. 15 to v. 35
23	June 3	— 9	..	72	„ 49 to v. 14	Matt. 17	2 Cor. 1 to v. 23
24	— 10	— 16	..	74	„ 51 to v. 17	Luke 9, v. 51	„ 4, v. 7, to 5, v. 11
25	— 17	— 23	..	77	„ 52 to v. 13	John 7 to v. 32	„ 9
26	— 24	— 30	..	78, v. 32	„ 52, v. 13, and 53	„ 8, v. 2 to v. 31	„ 13
27	July 1	July 7	..	80, 81	„ 54	„ 9 to v. 39	Gal. 5
28	— 8	— 14	..	84, 85	„ 55	Luke 10, v. 17 to v. 42	Eph. 1
29	— 15	— 21	..	87, 88	„ 58	„ 11, v. 29	„ 4, v. 25, to 5, v. 22
30	— 22	— 28	..	90	„ 59	„ 12, v. 32	„ 6, v. 10
31	— 29	Aug. 4	..	93, 94	„ 60	John 10, v. 22	Philip. 3
32	Aug. 5	— 11	..	97, 98	„ 61 and 62	Luke 13, v. 10	Col. 3, v. 5, to 4, v. 7
33	— 12	— 18	..	102	„ 63 and 64	„ 15	2 Thess. 1 and 2 to v. 13
34	— 19	— 25	..	104	„ 65	„ 17 to v. 20	1 Tim. 4
35	— 26	Sept. 1	..	106	„ 66	„ 18 to v. 15	„ 2 „ 3 to 4, v. 9
36	Sept. 2	— 8	..	108, 109	Jer. 1	Matt. 20 to v. 29	Philemon
37	— 9	— 15	..	112, 113	„ 5, v. 11	John 11, v. 55, and 12, v. 1, and v. 9 to v. 20	Heb. 4, v. 14, to 5, v. 11
38	— 16	— 22	..	116, 117	„ 7, v. 14, and 9	Matt. 21, v. 10 to v. 33	„ 11 to v. 17
39	— 23	— 29	..	119 to v. 17	„ 8, v. 14 to v. 18	„ 23	James 1
40	— 30	Oct. 6	..	119, v. 41 to v. 57	„ 13 to v. 18	Luke 21, v. 20 to v. 37	1 Pet. 1, or 1, v. 13, to 2, v. 11
41	Oct. 7	— 13	..	119, v. 81 to v. 97	„ 19 and 20 to v. 13	Matt. 25, v. 31	„ 5
42	— 14	— 20	..	119, v. 121 to v. 137	„ 23 to v. 23	John 13 to v. 21	2 Pet. 3
43	— 21	— 27	..	119, v. 161	„ 23, v. 23	Matt. 26, v. 26 to v. 36	1 John 3, v. 11
44	— 28	Nov. 3	..	123, 124, 125	„ 25	John 15 to v. 18	2 John
45	Nov. 4	— 10	..	128, 129	„ 26	„ 16, v. 5	Jude
46	— 11	— 17	..	132, 133	„ 27 or 28	Matt. 26, v. 36 to v. 57	Rev. 2 to v. 18
47	— 18	— 24	..	136	„ 30	„ 27 to v. 15	„ 3
48	— 25	Dec. 1	..	138	„ 31, v. 18	Luke 23, v. 6 to v. 26	„ 5
49	Dec. 2	— 8	..	140	„ 35	„ 23, v. 26 to v. 46	„ 7
50	— 9	— 15	..	143, 144	„ 36	John 20 to v. 19	„ 15
51	— 16	— 22	..	146	„ 38	Luke 24, v. 36 to v. 50	„ 18
52	— 23	— 29	..	148, 149, 150	„ 42 to 43, v. 8; or 50 to v. 21	John 21 to v. 15	„ 20
53	— 30	— 31	..	103	„ 51, v. 41; or Lamentations 2 to v. 20	Matt. 28, v. 16, and Mark 16, v. 9	„ 22

9

TABLE OF PSALMS AND LESSONS FOR DIVINE SERVICE ON EVERY LORD'S DAY THROUGHOUT THE YEAR.

SECOND YEAR.

Morning.

Lord's Day of the Year.	Month and Day.	Psalms.	Old Testament Lesson.	Gospel.	Epistle.
1	Jan. 1, 2, 3, 4, 5, 6, 7	1, 2	Josh. 3, v. 7, to 4, v. 15	Luke 1 to v. 26	Acts 1
2	— 8 Jan. 14	5, 6	„ 5, v. 10, to 6, v. 21	„ 1, v. 39 to v. 57	„ 2, v. 22
3	— 15 — 21	9	„ 7	Matt. 1, v. 18	„ 4 to v. 32
4	— 22 — 28	11, 12	„ 24	Luke 2, v. 21 to v. 40	„ 6, v. 9, to 7, v. 30
5	— 29 Feb. 4	15, 16	Judges 2	„ 2, v. 40	„ 9 to v. 31
6	Feb. 5 — 11	18 to v. 30	„ 6	„ 3	„ 10, v. 24
7	— 12 — 18	19	„ 7 to v. 23	John 1, v. 19 to v. 35	„ 12
8	— 19 — 25	22	„ 12 and 13	„ 2	„ 13, v. 14
9	— 26 Mar. 3	25	Ruth 1	„ 3, v. 22	„ 15 to v. 36
10	Mar. 4 — 10	28, 29	1 Sam. 3	„ 4, v. 43	„ 19, v. 23
11	— 11 — 17	32, 33	„ 4	Luke 4, v. 33	„ 21, v. 17 to 37
12	— 18 — 24	35	„ 9, v. 15, & 10 or 12	John 5 to v. 19	„ 23, v. 31, and 24
13	— 25 — 31	37	„ 15, v. 10, to 16, v. 14; or ch. 13	Matt. 12 to v. 22	„ 27
14	April 1 — 7	39, 40	„ 17, v. 12	Luke 6, v. 37	Rom. 1 to v. 18
15	— 8 — 14	42, 43	„ 24 or 26	„ 7, v. 11 to v. 35	„ 6
16	— 15 — 21	45	„ 28	„ 7, v. 36	„ 8, v. 18
17	— 22 — 28	47, 48	2 Sam. 1	„ 8 to v. 19	„ 12
18	— 29 May 5	50	„ 6	„ 8, v. 22 to v. 41	„ 14 to v. 19
19	May 6 — 12	52, 53	„ 12 to v. 24	Matt. 9, v. 35, to 10, v. 24	„ 16
20	— 13 — 19	56, 57	„ 15	John 6 to v. 22	1 Cor. 4
21	— 20 — 26	60, 61	„ 17	„ 6, v. 41, to 7, v. 2	„ 6
22	— 27 June 2	64, 65	„ 18	Matt. 15, v. 2 to 39	„ 10 to 11, v. 2

PSALMS AND LESSONS.

				Psalms			
23	June	June 3	June 9	68	2 Sam. 19 to v. 41	Matt. 16, v. 13	1 Cor. 12, v. 28, and 13
24	—	10	16	70, 71	1 Chron. 28 to v. 10, and 29	" 18 to 19, v. 2	" 15 to v. 35
25	July	17	23	73	2 Chron. 1 and 2	Luke 10 to v. 17	2 Cor. 1, v. 23, and 2
26	—	24	30	75, 76	1 Kings 6	John 7, v. 32, to 8, v. 2	" 5, v. 20, and 6 to 7, v. 2
27	July	July 1	July 7	78 to v. 32	" 8, v. 22	" 8, v. 31	" 10
28	—	8	14	79	" 11, v. 9	Luke 10, v. 17	Gal. 1
29	—	15	21	82, 83	" 12	" 11 to v. 29	" 4 to 5, v. 2
30	—	22	28	86	" 16, v. 29, and 17	" 12 to v. 32	Eph. 2, v. 19, and 3
31	—	29	Aug. 4	89	" 18	" 13 to v. 10	" 5, v. 8, to 6, v. 10
32	Aug.	Aug. 5	11	91, 92	" 19	John 11 to v. 46	Phil. 3, v. 17, and 4
33	—	12	18	95, 96	" 22 to v. 41	Luke 14	Col. 4
34	—	19	25	99, 100, 101	2 Kings 2 to v. 16	" 16	1 Thess. 2, v. 13, and 3
35	—	26	Sept. 1	103	" 4 or 5	" 17, v. 20	1 Tim. 2 and 3
36	Sept.	Sept. 2	8	105	" 10	Matt. 19	2 Tim. 1
37	—	9	15	107	" 13	Luke 19, v. 2 to v. 29	Titus 1
38	—	16	22	110, 111	" 17	John 12, v. 20	Philemon
39	—	23	29	114, 115	" 18, v. 37 (or v. 13 to v. 26), and 19	Mark 11, v. 27, to 12, v. 13	Heb. 5 to 6, v. 13
40	Oct.	30	Oct. 6	118	" 20	Matt. 23	" 10, v. 19
41	—	7	13	119, v. 17 to v. 41	2 Chron. 34, v. 8	" 24, v. 15	" 13, v. 5
42	—	14	20	119, v. 57 to v. 81	" 35	" 25, v. 31	James 4 or 5
43	—	21	27	119, v. 97 to v. 121	" 36	Luke 22 to v. 19	2 Peter 2
44	Nov.	28	Nov. 3	119, v. 137 to v. 161	Ezra 3	John 13, v. 21	1 John 5
45	—	4	10	120, 121, 122	Neh. 1 and 2	" 14	3 John
46	—	11	17	126, 127	" 7, v. 73, and viii.	" 16	Jude
47	—	18	24	130, 131	Esther 5, v. 9, 6 and 7	Luke 22, v. 39 to v. 54	Rev. 2 to v. 18
48	Dec.	25	Dec. 1	134, 135	Job 1 and 2 to v. 11	John 18, v. 28 to v. 39	" 3
49	—	Dec. 2	8	137, 138	" 2, v. 11, and 3	Matt. 27, v. 3 to v. 39	" 5
50	—	9	15	140, 141	" 8, v. 1 and v. 20, 21, 22, and ch. 9	" 28 to v. 16	" 7
51	—	16	22	144	" 11 to v. 7, ch. 12 and 13 to v. 17, or ch. 28	Luke 24, v. 13 to v. 36	" 12
52	—	23	29	147	" 38	John 20, v. 19 to v. 31	" 19
53	—	30	31	31, 39	" 42	" 21, v. 15	" 21

TABLE OF PSALMS AND LESSONS FOR DIVINE SERVICE ON EVERY LORD'S DAY THROUGHOUT THE YEAR.

SECOND YEAR.

Evening.

Lord's Day of the Year.	Month and Day.	Psalms.	Old Testament Lesson.	Gospel.	Epistle.
1	Jan. 1, 2, 3, 4, 5, 6, 7	3, 4	Ezek. 1 and 2	Luke 1, v. 26 to v. 39	Acts 2 to v. 22
2	— 8 Jan. 14	7, 8	" 3	" 1, v. 57	" 3
3	— 15 — 21	10	" 8 and 9	" 2 to v. 21	" 4, v. 32, to 5, v. 17
4	— 22 — 28	13, 14	" 10	Matt. 2	" 7, v. 30
5	— 29 Feb. 4	17	" 11	John 1 to v. 19	" 10 to v. 24
6	Feb. 5 — 11	18, v. 30	" 14	Luke 4 to v. 15	" 11
7	— 12 — 18	20, 21	" 17	John 1, v. 35	" 13 to v. 14
8	— 19 — 25	23, 24	" 20, v. 30	" 3 to v. 22	" 14
9	— 26 Mar. 3	26, 27	" 24	" 4, v. 4 to v. 43	" 18
10	Mar. 4 — 10	30, 31	" 26	Luke 4, v. 16 to v. 33	" 20
11	— 11 — 17	34	" 27	" 5, v. 12 to v. 27	" 21, v. 37, to 22, v. 30
12	— 18 — 24	36	" 33 to v. 21	John 5, v. 19	" 26
13	— 25 — 31	38	" 34	Luke 6, v. 12 to v. 37	" 28
14	April 1 — 7	41	" 36, v. 19	Matt. 8 to v. 14	Rom. 3, v. 19, to 4, v. 9
15	— 8 — 14	44	" 37	" 11, v. 20	" 7, v. 21, to 8, v. 18
16	— 15 — 21	46	" 39, v. 17	Mark 3, v. 22	" 11, v. 22
17	— 22 — 28	49	" 43 to 44, v. 5	" 4, v. 26	" 13
18	— 29 May 5	51	" 47 to v. 13	Luke 8, v. 41	" 14, v. 19, to 15, v. 14
19	May 6 — 12	54, 55	Dan. 1	Matt. 10, v. 24	1 Cor. 3
20	— 13 — 19	58, 59	" 2	John 6, v. 22 to v. 41	" 5

PSALMS AND LESSONS.

			Psalms	Lessons	Lessons
21	May 20	May 26			1 Cor. 9
22	" 27	June 2	62, 63 / 66, 67		" 12 to v. 28
23	June 3	June 9	69	Dan. 3	" 14, v. 20
24	" 10	" 16	72	" 4	" 15, v. 35
25	" 17	" 23	74	" 5	2 Cor. 3 to 4, v. 7
26	" 24	" 30	77	" 6	" 8
27	July 1	July 7	78, v. 32	" 7	" 13
28	" 8	" 14	80, 81 / 84, 85	" 8	Gal. 2
29	" 15	" 21	87, 88	" 9	Eph. 2 to v. 19
30	" 22	" 28	90	" 10	" 4, v. 17, to 5, v. 8
31	" 29	Aug. 4	93, 94 / 97, 98	" 11, v. 36, and 12	Phil. 1, v. 27, to 2, v. 19
32	Aug. 5	" 11	102	Hosea 5, v. 8, to 6, v. 7	Col. 2, v. 6, to 3, v. 5
33	" 12	" 18	104	" 10, v. 12, and 11	1 Thess. 1 to 2, v. 13
34	" 19	" 25	106	" 13, v. 9, and 14	2 Thess. 2, v. 13, and 3
35	" 26	Sept. 1	108, 109	Joel 2	1 Tim. 6
36	Sept. 2	" 8	112, 113	" 3 v. 9	2 Tim. 4
37	" 9	" 15	116, 117	Amos 5 to v. 18	Titus 3
38	" 16	" 22	119 to v. 17	Obadiah	Heb. 3 to 4, v. 12
39	" 23	" 29	119, v. 41 to v. 57	Jonah 1 and 2	" 8
40	" 30	Oct. 6	119, v. 81 to v. 97	Micah 3 and 4 to v. 9	" 11, v. 17, to 12, v. 3
41	Oct. 7	" 13	119, v. 121 to v. 137	Nahum 1	James 2
42	" 14	" 20		Hab. 1 and 2 to v. 15	1 Pet. 3, v. 13, to 4, v. 12
43	" 21	" 27	119, v. 161	Zeph. 1 to 2, v. 4	1 John 2, v. 15, to 3, v. 11
44	" 28	Nov. 3	123, 124, 125	Haggai 2	2 John
45	Nov. 4	" 10	128, 129	Zech. 1	3 John
46	" 11	" 17	132, 133	" 8 to v. 18	Rev. 1
47	" 18	" 24	136	" 10	" 2, v. 18
48	" 25	Dec. 1	139	" 11	" 4
49	Dec. 2	" 8	142, 143	" 12 to 13, v. 7	" 6
50	" 9	" 15	145, 146	" 14	" 10 and 11
51	" 16	" 22	148, 149, 150	Mal. 1	" 13 to 14, v. 5
52	" 23	" 29	102	" 2	" 20
53	" 30	" 31		" 3 and 4	" 22

TABLE OF LESSONS FOR A THIRD SERVICE.*

Lord's Day of the Year.	Month and Day.	FIRST YEAR.		SECOND YEAR.	
		First Lesson.	Second Lesson.	First Lesson.	Second Lesson.
1	Jan. 1, 2, 3, 4, 5, 6, 7	Isaiah 40	Matt. 1, v. 18, and 2	Isaiah 43	Luke 1 to v. 39
2	— 8 Jan. 14	Ezekiel 28	„ 3	Micah 4	1, v. 39
3	— 15 — 21	Jeremiah 16, v. 9	„ 4	Ezra 10 to v. 17	2
4	— 22 — 28	Isaiah 1, v. 18	„ 5 to v. 21	Nehemiah 9	3 to v. 23
5	— 29 Feb. 4	Amos 8	„ 5, v. 21	Isaiah 50	4
6	Feb. 5 — 11	Jeremiah 3, v. 11	„ 6	„ 30 v. 12	5
7	— 12 — 18	„ 33	„ 7	„ 31	6
8	— 19 — 25	Zephaniah 3	„ 8	Proverbs 23 to v. 26	7
9	— 26 Mar. 3	Jeremiah 2 to v. 20	„ 9	„ 18, v. 10	8 to v. 26
10	Mar. 4 — 10	Zechariah 9	„ 10	Isaiah 39	8, v. 26
11	— 11 — 17	Jeremiah 4 to v. 19	„ 11	Lamentations 1 to v. 17	9 to v. 28
12	— 18 — 24	Ezekiel 16, v. 44	„ 12 to v. 22	Ezekiel 18, v. 20	9, v. 28
13	— 25 — 31	Proverbs 3 to v. 27	„ 12, v. 22	Proverbs 21	10
14	April 1 — 7	Daniel, 9 to v. 5, and from v. 16	„ 13 to v. 31	„ 12	11 to v. 29
15	— 8 — 14	Proverbs 19	„ 13, v. 31	Proverbs 24 to v. 23	11, v. 29
16	— 15 — 21	Micah 6, v. 9, to 7, v. 10	„ 14	Job 4	12 to v. 35
17	— 22 — 28	Job 33, v. 14	„ 15	„ 14	12, v. 35
18	— 29 May 5	Hosea 11, v. 12, and 12	„ 16	Ezekiel 2	13
19	May 6 — 12	Jeremiah 31 to v. 18	„ 17	Jeremiah 18 to v. 18	14
20	— 13 — 19	Job 5	„ 18	Job 19	15
21	— 20 — 26	„ 10	„ 19 to v. 27	„ 22	16
22	— 27 June 2	Lament. 3, v. 22 to v. 42	„ 19, v. 27, and 20	Proverbs 28	17

LESSONS FOR A THIRD SERVICE.

#	Date	Lesson		Ref		Date	Lesson		Ref	
23	June 3	June 9	Isaiah 10, v. 5 to v. 28	..	21 to v. 23	..	Proverbs 29	..	18	..
24	— 10	— 16	Ecclesiastes 8 to v. 14	..	21, v. 23	..	Isaiah 32	..	19	..
25	— 17	— 23	Isaiah 49, v. 14	..	22	..	Ecclesiastes 9	..	20	..
26	— 24	— 30	Ezek. 38, v. 14, to 39 v. 11	..	23	..	Ezra 6	..	21	..
27	July 1	July 7	" 13 to v. 17	..	24	..	Isaiah 56 to 57, v. 3	..	22 to v. 39	..
28	— 8	— 14	" 9	..	25	..	Ecclesiastes 10	..	22, v. 39	..
29	— 15	— 21	Habakkuk 3	..	26 to v. 36	..	Jeremiah 10	..	23	..
30	— 22	— 28	Hosea 2, v. 14	..	26, v. 36	..	" 15	..	24	..
31	— 29	Aug. 4	Isaiah 48	..	27 to v. 32	..	Job 28	..	John 1	..
32	Aug. 5	— 11	Malachi 3, v. 13, and 4	..	27, v. 32	..	" 23	..	2	..
33	— 12	— 18	Haggai 1	..	28	..	Isaiah 30 to v. 18	..	3	..
34	— 19	— 25	Zechariah 6, v. 9, and 7	..	Mark 1	..	Micah 2	..	4	..
35	— 26	Sept. 1	Malachi 1 to v. 12	..	2	..	Zechariah 4	..	5	..
36	Sept. 2	— 8	Isaiah 64	..	3	..	Jeremiah 17 to v. 19	..	6 to v. 22	..
37	— 9	— 15	" 60, v. 13	..	4	..	Amos 5, v. 18, to 6, v. 9	..	6, v. 22	..
38	— 16	— 22	Joel 1	..	5	..	Isaiah 7 to v. 17	..	7	..
39	— 23	— 29	Hosea 4 to v. 11	..	6 to v. 30	..	" 27, or 30, v. 25	..	8, to v. 21	..
40	— 30	Oct. 6	Jeremiah 14	..	6, v. 30	..	" 38, v. 9	..	8, v. 21	..
41	Oct. 7	— 13	Nahum 1 or Isaiah 61	..	7	..	" 48, v. 9	..	9 v. 39	..
42	— 14	— 20	Song of Solomon, 2, or Ezekiel 20 to v. 27	..	8	..	Jeremiah 22 to v. 20	..	9, v. 39, and 10	..
43	— 21	— 27	Ezekiel 44 to v. 17	..	9 to v. 30	..	" 24	..	11 to v. 54	..
44	— 28	Nov. 3	Zechariah 3	..	9, v. 30	..	Ezra 8	..	11, v. 54, and 12	..
45	Nov. 4	— 10	Amos 9	..	10 to v. 32	..	Nehemiah 4	..	13	..
46	— 11	— 17	Proverbs 26	..	10, v. 32	..	Isaiah 61	..	14	..
47	— 18	— 24	Jonah 3 and 4	..	11	..	Proverbs 11	..	15	..
48	— 25	Dec. 1	Micah 6 to v. 9	..	12	..	Jeremiah 12	..	16	..
49	Dec. 2	— 8	Lament. 1 to v. 16	..	13	..	Isaiah 57, v. 10	..	17	..
50	— 9	— 15	Isaiah 50	..	14 to v. 32	..	" 50	..	18 to v. 28	..
51	— 16	— 22	Proverbs 4	..	14, v. 32	..	Job 29	..	18, v. 28, to 19, v. 31	..
52	— 23	— 29	Proverbs 4	..	15	..	" 39 to 40, v. 6, or Jeremiah 45	..	19, v. 31, and 20	..
53	— 30	—	Ezekiel 12	..	16	..	Hosea 14	..	21	..

* This Table may be used on the Lord's Day when there are three Services, or at any Week-day Service. The Psalms appointed are those proper to the day of the month.

Table

of

Selected Portions of the Psalms, Paraphrases, and Hymns

TABLE OF SELECTED PORTIONS OF THE PSALMS
(METRICAL VERSION),
PARAPHRASES, AND HYMNS.

For Opening of Divine Service.	For Opening of Divine Service.	For Chanting.	For Chanting.	For Chanting.
Ps. 3, omitting v. 7	Ps. 126	Ps. 2	Ps. 76	Par. 1
" 9, v. 7 to v. 12	" 130	" 4	" 77, v. 1 to v. 13, or v. 13 to end	" 2
" 15	" 133	" 5		" 6
" 19, v. 1 to v. 7	" 138, v. 1 to v. 6	" 6 (2d version)	" 79, v. 5	" 9
" 20, v. 1 to v. 6	" 139, v. 1 to v. 7	" 8	" 80, v. 8	" 18
" 22, v. 23 to v. 27	" 139, v. 7 to v. 13	" 11	" 81, v. 8	" 19
" 24, v. 7	" 143, v. 6 to v. 12	" 13	" 84	" 20
" 25, v. 1 to v. 7	" 145, v. 1 to v. 7	" 16	" 85	" 22
" 26, v. 6 to v. 9, & v. 12	" 145, v. 17	" 18, v. 6 to v. 20	" 86, v. 8	" 23
" 27, v. 4 to v. 7	" 147, v. 1 to v. 6	" 18, v. 28 to v. 37	" 89, v. 1 to v. 9	" 24
" 30, v. 1 to v. 5	" 148 (2d version)	" 19	" 89, v. 7 to v. 19	" 25
" 33, v. 1 to v. 6	" 149, v. 1 to v. 5	" 20	" 89, v. 19 to v. 30, or v. 38	" 26, v. 5
" 34, v. 1 to v. 8	Par. 2	" 21, v. 1 to v. 8, & v. 13		" 30
" 36, v. 5 to v. 10	" 18, v. 1 to v. 5	" 22, v. 22	" 90, v. 8	" 32
" 45, v. 2 to v. 7	" 20, v. 1 to v. 5	" 23	" 91	" 33
" 46, v. 1 to v. 6	" 26, v. 1 to v. 5	" 24	" 92, v. 6	" 34
" 51, v. 14 to v. 18	" 27	" 25, v. 1, or v. 9 to v. 16	" 95	" 36
" 57, v. 1 to v. 4	" 30	" 26	" 96, v. 6	" 37
" 60, v. 1 to v. 6	" 32	" 27, v. 1 to v. 7, or v. 7 to v. 14	" 97	" 38, v. 4
" 61, v. 1 to v. 5	" 57, v. 1 to v. 5, or v. 3 to end	" 28	" 98	" 39
" 62, v. 5 to v. 9		" 29	" 99	" 41
" 63, v. 1 to v. 6	" 58	" 30, v. 4	" 102, v. 12	" 48
" 65, v. 1 to v. 5	" 61	" 31, v. 1 to v. 9, or v. 19 to end	" 103, v. 1 to v. 13, or v. 13 to end	" 49, v. 5 to v. 14
" 67	" 65, v. 1 to v. 5			" 50
" 68, v. 1 to v. 6	Hymn 1		" 104, v. 1 to v. 10	" 51, to v. 9

TABLE OF PORTIONS OF PSALMS, &c.

" 2	" 32, v. 1 to v. 8	" 105, v. 1 to v. 11	" 52
" 3	" 33, v. 1 to v. 10	" 107, v. 1 to v. 16, or v. 21 to v. 32	" 53
" 4	" 34, v. 8 to v. 20		" 56
" 9	" 37, v. 3 to v. 12	" 110	" 57
" 12	" 37, v. 29 to end	" 111	" 62
" 31	" 39, v. 4	" 112	" 65
" 32	" 40, v. 5 to v. 12	" 113	" 66
" 34	" 41	" 114	" 67
" 61	" 42	" 115	
" 73	" 45, v. 1 to v. 12, or v. 10 to end	" 116, v. 1 to v. 9, or v. 9 to end	The following invitatory Psalms may be used when there is a celebration of the Lord's Supper.
" 74	" 46	" 118, v. 1 to v. 15, or v. 15 to end	
" 75	" 47		
" 77	" 48	" 119, v. 25 to v. 33	
" 78	" 50, v. 1, or v. 7 to v. 16	" 119, v. 57 to v. 65	
" 167	" 51, v. 1 to v. 14, or v. 8 to end	" 119, v. 89 to v. 97	Ps. 22, v. 23 to v. 27
" 168		" 119, v. 105 to v. 113	" 23
" 169	" 53	" 119, v. 129 to v. 137	" 24, v. 1 to v. 6, or v. 7 to end
" 190	" 55, v. 1 to v. 10, or v. 12 to end	" 122	" 26, v. 6 to v. 9, & v. 12
" 191	" 56	" 124	" 43, v. 3
" 192	" 57	" 132, v. 7 to end	" 50, v. 1 to v. 7
" 193	" 61	" 135, v. 1 to v. 8, and v. 20, 21	" 63, v. 1 to v. 6
" 194	" 62, v. 5	" 136, v. 1 to v. 17, and v. 23 to end	" 106, v. 1 to v. 6
" 195	" 63		" 116, v. 13
	" 65, v. 5	" 137	" 118, v. 19 to v. 27
	" 66	" 138	" 118, v. 24
	" 67 (2d version)	" 139, v. 7 to v. 18	" 132, v. 7 to v. 11
	" 68, v. 1 to v. 11, or v. 16 to v. 25	" 142	" 132, v. 11 to v. 17
	" 69, v. 1 to v. 10	" 144, v. 9	" 136 (2d version), v. 1 to v. 5, and v. 23 to end
	" 71, v. 1 to v. 16	" 145, v. 8	
	" 72, v. 7	" 146, v. 6	" 146, v. 5
" 68, v. 7 to v. 11	" 74, v. 1 to v. 12	" 147, v. 6	
" 69, v. 30, and v. 33 to end	" 75	" 148	
" 71, v. 20		" 149	
" 73, v. 23 to v. 27			
" 80, v. 1 to v. 5			
" 84, v. 1 to v. 4			
" 84, v. 8			
" 85, v. 8			
" 86			
" 89, v. 6 to v. 9			
" 89, v. 15 to v. 19			
" 90, v. 13 to end			
" 92, v. 1 to v. 5			
" 93			
" 95, v. 1 to v. 7			
" 96, v. 1 to v. 7			
" 96, v. 9 to end			
" 98, v. 1 to v. 5			
" 100			
" 102, v. 13 to v. 19			
" 103, v. 1 to v. 6			
" 103, v. 13 to v. 19			
" 103, v. 19			
" 104, v. 1 to v. 6			
" 105, v. 1 to v. 7			
" 107, v. 1 to v. 9			
" 108, v. 1 to v. 7			
" 115, v. 12			
" 116, v. 1 to v. 8			
" 121			
" 122, v. 1 to v. 7			
" 123			
" 124			
" 125			

Table

of

Psalms and Lessons

for

Special Services

TABLE OF PSALMS AND LESSONS FOR SPECIAL SERVICES.

	MORNING.	EVENING.		MORNING.	EVENING.
Last day of the Year 1st Lesson	Deuteronomy 8	Ecclesiastes 3, v. 1 to 16	Commemoration of the Nativity* 1st Lesson	Isaiah 9, v. 2 to 8; or 7, v. 10 to 17; or Micah 4, v. 8, to 5, v. 5	Isaiah 11 and 12
2d Lesson	Matthew 24, v. 36; 2 Peter 3	Luke 12, v. 13 to 49; Romans 13, v. 8	2d Lesson	Luke 2, v. 1 to 21; Heb. 1, v. 1 to 13	John 1, v. 1 to 19; Hebrews 2
Psalms	90, 91, 103	39, 31	Psalms	84, 85	132, 148, 149, 150
First Day of Year 1st Lesson	Deut. 11; or Exodus, 33, v. 1 to 20	1 Chronicles 29, v. 1 to 26; or Joshua 1, v. 1 to 10	Commemoration of the Crucifixion† 1st Lesson	Isaiah 52, v. 13, and 53; or Lev. 16	Micah 7, v. 1 to 9; or Isaiah 50
2d Lesson	Matthew 25, v. 1 to 31; Romans 12	John 21, v. 15; 1 Thessalonians 5; or James 4, v. 13, to 5, v. 9	2d Lesson	Heb. 10, v. 1 to 25; Matt. 26, v. 36, to 27, v. 55	John 19, v. 1 to 37; 2 Corinthians 5, v. 11
Psalms	19, 20, 95, 96	26, 27	Psalms	51, 22, 40	88, 140, 141, 142

* Lessons appropriate at Preparatory Services. † Preparatory Services.

	MORNING.	EVENING.		MORNING.	EVENING.
1.—1st Lesson	Isaiah 1	Isaiah 11; or 4, v. 2	1.—1st Lesson	Zechariah 9, v. 9; Luke 19, v. 29; or Matt. 21, v. 1 to 17	Zechariah 11
2d Lesson	Matthew 21, v. 1 to 14; Rom. 13, v. 8	Matt. 25, 46	2d Lesson	Phil. 2, v. 1 to 12	
Psalms			Psalms	124, 125, 126	
2.—1st Lesson	Isaiah 5	Isaiah 11, to v. 11; or 21	2.—1st Lesson	Lam. 1, v. 1 to 15	Matthew 16
2d Lesson	Luke 21, v. 25 to 31; Rom. 15, v. 4 to 14	Matt. 5, to v. 21	2d Lesson	Matt. 21, v. 18 to 28	
Psalms	9	10, 11	Psalms	119, v. 1 to 17	129, 130, 131
3.—1st Lesson	Isaiah 25	Isaiah 26; or 28, v. 6 to 19	3.—1st Lesson	Lamentations 3, v. 1 to 24	Lam. 2, v. 1 to 20; Luke 20, or Matt. 22
2d Lesson	Matt. 11, v. 2 to 16; 1 Cor. 4, v. 1 to 6	John 14	2d Lesson	Matthew 23	119, v. 17 to 41; Lamentations 3, v. 1 to 42; or Gen. 22
Psalms	49	50	Psalms	119, v. 41 to 65; Lam. 3, v. 42	Luke 21; or Matt. 24; or John 12, v. 20 to 42
4.—1st Lesson	Isaiah 32	Isaiah 33, v. 2 to 23	4.—1st Lesson	Matthew 25	Daniel 9, v. 20; or Exodus 24
2d Lesson	John 1, v. 19 to 29; Phil. 4, v. 4 to 10	John 16	2d Lesson	119, v. 89 to 105; Exodus 12	Matt. 26, v. 1 to 17; 119, v. 105 to 129
Psalms	97, 98	99	5.—1st Lesson	Luke 22, v. 1 to 54; or John 13	John 14, 15, 16, and 17
			2d Lesson	119, v. 129 to 153	119, v. 153

PSALMS AND LESSONS FOR SPECIAL SERVICES.

TABLE OF PSALMS AND LESSONS FOR SPECIAL SERVICES.

		MORNING.	EVENING.			MORNING.	EVENING.
Commemoration of the Resurrection *	1st Lesson	Isa. 25; or Exod. 14	Isaiah 26	Preparation for the Holy Communion.	1st Lesson	Exodus 16	Exod. 20, v. 1 to 22
	2d Lesson	{ Colossians 3, v. 1 to 6 { John 20, v. 1 to 21	{ Matthew 28; or { Luke 24, v. 1 to 36 { Rev. 1, v. 1 to 19; { or Rev. 5		2d Lesson	{ John 6, v. 1 to 41 { 1 Corinthians 10, { v. 1 to 22	{ Matthew 5, v. 1 to 17 { 2 Corinthians 13
	Psalms	9, 110, 111, 72; or 148, 149, 150	113, 114, 118		Psalms	25, 26	138, 139, 122
Commemoration of the Ascension	1st Lesson	2 Kings 2; or Exod. 24	Isaiah 49, v. 13	Or	1st Lesson	1 Kings 19, v. 1 to 9	Exodus 19, v. 1 to 14
	2d Lesson	{ Ephesians 1 { Luke 24, v. 36	{ Acts 1, v. 1 to 12 { Hebrews 4		2d Lesson	{ John 6, v. 41 to 64 { 1 Corinthians 11, v. 18	{ Matthew 7, v. 21 { Hebrows 12, v. 14
	Psalms	20, 21, 45; or 148, 149, 150	8, 24, 46, 47		Psalms	42, 43, 121	141, 142
Commemoration of the Descending of the Holy Ghost †	1st Lesson	Isaiah 60	Isaiah 61	″	1st Lesson	Genesis 14, v. 8	Deuteronomy 6
	2d Lesson	{ Ephesians 4, to v. 17 { Acts 11	{ Acts 19, v. 1 to 21 { Ephesians 4, v. 17; { or Gal. 5, v. 16		2d Lesson	{ Matthew 26, v. 17 { Hebrews 13 v. 10	{ Matt. 13, v. 1 to 24 { Galatians 5, v. 13, { to 6, v. 6
	Psalms	48, 68, 132, 133; or 148, 149, 150	104, 145		Psalms	34, 72	132, 133, 134
				″	1st Lesson	Exodus 12, v. 1 to 20	Joshua 24, v. 14
					2d Lesson	{ Mark 14, v. 1 to 27 { 1 Corinthians 5, v. 6	{ Luke 14, v. 16 { 1 Peter 1, v. 1 to 12
					Psalms	84, 85	137, 138

	1st Lesson	* Preparatory Services.	Jonah 2		1st Lesson	† Preparatory Service. Isaiah 58; or 1 Kings 18, v. 17 to 40	Joel 2, v. 15
	2d Lesson	{ 1 Pet. 3, v. 17, to 4, v. 12 { Matthew 27, v. 57	{ Romans 6 to v. 14 { Mark 15, v. 42		2d Lesson	{ Acts 1, v. 12 { John 14, v. 15 to 29	{ John 10, v. 5 to 17; or { 1 Peter 1, v. 10
	Psalms	Hosea 5, v. 8 to 6, v. 4; or 13, v. 14, to 14, v. 4 27, 28, 4	16, 17, 30, 31		Psalms	62, 63, 119, v. 17 to 33	84, 85, 119, v. 33 to 49

TABLE OF PSALMS AND LESSONS FOR SPECIAL SERVICES.

		MORNING.	EVENING.			MORNING.	EVENING.
Preparation for the Holy Communion	1st Lesson 2d Lesson Psalms	Isaiah 55 Luke 22, v. 1 to 31 Acts 20, v. 7 86, 87	Nehemiah 8 Mark 5, v. 21 Acts 27, v. 21 100, 101	Humiliation for Sins	1st Lesson 2d Lesson Psalms	Isaiah 59 Luke 6, v. 20 1 John 1, v. 6, to 2, v. 3 38, 39, 51	Hosea 14 Luke 18, v. 1 to 15 2 Corinthians 7, v. 5 to 12 25, 57, 40
Or	1st Lesson 2d Lesson Psalms	Malachi 1 John 13 Jude v. 11 73, 74	2 Chron. 30, v. 13 Matt. 22, v. 1 to 15 Rev. 19, v. 1 to 11 64, 65	Humiliation under Calamity	1st Lesson	Dan. 9; or 2 Chron. 6, v. 18 to 42, and 7, v. 12 to 17; or Deut. 4, v. 23 to 41; or Lev. 26, v. 14; or Isa. 3 or 34 Or, in time of Sickness, 2 Sam. 24, v. 10; Num. 16, v. 44; or 2 Kings 5 Or, in time of Scarcity, Gen. 8, v. 15; or Exod. 16; or Exod. 17, v. 1 to 8; or 1 Kings 18; or Jer. 14; or Joel 1, v. 7 Or, in time of War, 2 Chron. 14; or 32, v. 1 to 24; 2 Chron. 20, v. 1 to 22; or Exod. 17, v. 8; or Deut. 20	Jonah 3 and 4
"	1st Lesson 2d Lesson Psalms	Isaiah 52 Matt. 27, v. 20 to 55 Hebrews 9 116, 117	1 Chronicles 16 Matthew 11, v. 16 Acts 2, v. 29 15, 16				
"	1st Lesson 2d Lesson Psalms	Isaiah 53 Mark 15, v. 1 to 40 Heb. 10, v. 1 to 26 118	Ezekiel 18, v. 19 Matt. 8, v. 1 to 18 2 Corinthians 7 62, 63				
"	1st Lesson 2d Lesson Psalms	Isaiah 58 Luke 23, v. 18 Revelation 3, v. 7 124, 125, 126	Ezekiel 34, v. 11 John 10, v. 1 to 30 Rev. 14, v. 1 to 6 23, 24				
"	1st Lesson 2d Lesson Psalms	Isaiah 12 John 19, v. 1 to 31 Revelation 5, v. 6 130, 131, 132	Malachi 3 Mark 6, v. 30 Revelation 22 80, 81				

TABLE OF PSALMS AND LESSONS FOR SPECIAL SERVICES.

	Morning.	Evening.		Morning.	Evening.
Humiliation under Calamity 2d Lesson	Matt. 21, v. 17 to 23; or 24 Or, in time of Sickness, Matt. 8, v. 1 to 18; or John 5. v. 1 to 16 Or, in time of Scarcity, Matt. 6, v. 25; or Mark 8, v. 1 to 10; or John 7, v. 5 to 14 Or, in time of War, James 4, v. 1 to 11; or 1 Thess. 5	Matthew 14, v. 22 to 34 Hebrews 12, v. 1 to 14; or 1 Peter 4	In time of Rejoicing 2d Lesson	Luke 19, v. 28 to 41 Philippians 4	Matt. 7, v. 7 to 14 1 Thessalonians 5. v. 14; or Rev. 5
			Psalms	92, 104, 105, 118, 136, 144, 147	103, 107, 116, 148
			Rejoicing for Victory and Peace 1st Lesson	Exod. 15, v. 1 to 19; or 2 Sam. 22; or Isa. 11, or 35, or 60; or Micah 4	
Psalms	In time of Sickness, 6, 49, 38, 39 In time of Scarcity, 73, 51, 57 In time of War, 2, 7, 17, 27, 44. 46, 60, 144	88, 143 102 108, 119, 144	2d Lesson Psalms	Revelation 21 Romans 12 46, 115, 124, 66, 67, 84	
			Thanksgiving for Harvest 1st Lesson	Deuteronomy 8 or 11; or 26, v. 1 to 12; or 28, v. 1 to 15; or 32, v. 7 to 20; or 33, v. 7; or Hosea 2, v. 14	
In time of Rejoicing 1st Lesson	Lev. 26, v. 1 to 14; or Num. 24; or 1 Kings 3, v. 5 to 15; or 2 Kings 18, v. 1 to 8; or 1 Chron. 17, v. 16; or 2 Chron. 30	Isaiah 25	2d Lesson Psalms	Matt. 13, v. 24 to 44; or John 4, v. 31 to 39; or 6, v. 26 to 36; or 2 Cor. 9, v. 6; or Rom. 12; or Rev. 14, v. 13 55, 100, 147, 65, 126, 127, 128, 144, 145	

TABLE OF PSALMS AND LESSONS FOR SPECIAL SERVICES.

	MORNING.	EVENING.		MORNING.	EVENING.
Ordination of Presbyters and their induction to Office			Missionary Services		
1st Lesson	Isa. 6, v. 1 to 9; or 35, or 40, v. 1 to 12; or 49, or 52, v. 7 to end; or 61, or 62; or Ezek. 33, v. 1 to 10		1st Lesson	Numbers 14, v. 1 to 22; or Isa. 42, v. 1 to 17, or 49, or 60, or 61, or 66, v. 5; or Jer. 33; or Ezek. 37 or 39; or Zeph. 3; or Zech. 8, v. 20 & 9	
2d Lesson	Matt. 28; or Luke 10, v. 1 to 25; or John 10, v. 1 to 17; or Acts 20, v. 17; or 1 Cor. 2, or 3, or 4; Eph. 4, v. 1 to 17; 1 Tim. 3, v. 1 to 8; or 2 Tim. 3 and 4, to v. 9; or 1 Pet. 5		2d Lesson	John 4, v. 20 to 37; or Matt. 28; or Luke 10, v. 1 to 19; or John 17; or Rom. 10, or 11; or 1 Tim. 2, v. 1 to 0; or Eph. 3; or Rev. 7, or 14, or 21, v. 9 to 22, v. 6	
Psalms	23, 67, 72, 80, 88, 89, 96, 98, 117, 121, 172		Psalms Opening or Dedication of Churches	2, 45, 72, 80, 96, 122	
Admission to the Office of Deacon			1st Lesson	1 Kings 8, v. 22; or 1 Chronicles 29	
1st Lesson	Isaiah 35, or 41, to v. 15; or Exodus 18, or 23, to v. 14		2d Lesson	Mark 11, v. 11 { Heb. 10, v. 19 to 26 24, 27, 45, 46, 47, 48, 84	
2d Lesson	{ Luke 12, v. 35 to 49 { Acts 6, v. 1 to 9 1 Tim. 3, v. 8 to 14		Psalms Reopening of Churches after Restoration		
Psalms	122, 112, 113		1st Lesson	2 Chronicles 34, v. 8 to 29; or Ezra 3; or Haggai 2	

TABLE OF PSALMS AND LESSONS FOR SPECIAL SERVICES.

	MORNING.	EVENING.	MORNING.	EVENING.
Reopening of Churches after Restoration 1st Lesson	Luke 19, v. 37; or John 2, v. 13			
2d Lesson	Eph. 2; or Rev. 18			
Psalms	87, 100, 118, 122, 133, 134, 150			
Children's Festivals 1st Lesson	Proverbs 3 or 4; or Ecclesiastes 12			
2d Lesson	Luke 2, v. 40 Eph. 5, v. 15, to 6, v. 21; or 2 Tim. 3			
Psalms	8, 23, 34, 148			
At a Meeting of Presbytery, Synod, or General Assembly 1st Lesson	Isaiah 61; or Ezek. 3, v. 10; or 34, v. 7; Malachi 2, v. 1 to 8			
At a Meeting of Presbytery, Synod, or General Assembly 2d Lesson			Gospel: Matt. 17, v. 1 to 21; or John 13, v. 1 to 18; or John 19, v. 1 to 17; or John 20, v. 19 to 24; or John 21, v. 15 to 23	
			Epistle: Acts 20, v. 17; or 1 Cor. 3; or 2 Cor. 4 or 6; or Eph. 4, v. 1 to 17; or 2 Tim. 1, or 2, or 3, or 4, v. 1 to 19; or 1 Peter 4, v. 7 to 12; or Rev. 2 or 3	
Psalms			68, 84, 87, 102, 122, 133, 148, 149, 150	

Table

of

Daily Lessons

TABLE OF DAILY LESSONS.—January hath 31 Days.

	Morning.		Evening.	
	First Lesson.	Second Lesson.	First Lesson.	Second Lesson.
1	Genesis 1 to 2, v. 4	Matthew 1	Genesis 2, v. 4	Acts 1
2	" 3	" 2	" 4	" 2 to v. 22
3	" 5 to v. 28	" 3	" 5, v. 28, to 6, v. 9	" 2, v. 22
4	" 6, v. 9, to 7, v. 11	" 4 to v. 23	" 7, v. 11, to 8, v. 13	" 3
5	" 8, v. 13 to 9, v. 20	" 4, v. 23, to 5, v. 13	" 10 to 11, v. 10	" 4 to v. 32
6	" 11, v. 27, and 12	" 5, v. 13 to v. 27	" 13	" 4, v. 32, to 5, v. 17
7	" 14	" 5, v. 27, to 6, v. 19	" 15	" 5, v. 17
8	" 16	" 6, v. 19	" 17 to v. 23	" 6
9	" 18	" 7	" 19, v. 12 to v. 30	" 7 to v. 35
10	" 20	" 8 to v. 18	" 21	" 7, v. 35, to 8, v. 5
11	" 22 to v. 20	" 8, v. 18	" 23	" 8, v. 5 to v. 26
12	" 24, v. 1 to v. 29	" 9 to v. 18	" 24, v. 29	" 8, v. 26
13	" 25	" 9, v. 18	" 26	" 9 to v. 23
14	" 27 to v. 41	" 10 to v. 24	" 27, v. 41, and 28	" 9, v. 23
15	" 29 to v. 21	" 10, v. 24, to 11, v. 2	" 31 to v. 25	" 10 to v. 24
16	" 31, v. 36	" 11, v. 2	" 32	" 10, v. 24
17	" 33	" 12 to v. 22	" 35 to v. 21	" 11 to v. 27
18	" 37	" 12, v. 22	" 39	" 11, v. 27, and 12
19	" 40	" 13 to v. 24	" 41 to v. 37	" 13 to v. 14
20	" 41, v. 37	" 13, v. 24 to v. 53	" 42	" 13, v. 14 to v. 44
21	" 43 to v. 25	" 13, v. 53, to 14, v. 13	" 43, v. 25, to 44, v. 14	" 13, v. 44, to 14, v. 8
22	" 44, v. 14	" 14, v. 13	" 45 to 46, v. 8	" 14, v. 8
23	" 46, v. 26, to 47, v. 13	" 15 to v. 21	" 47, v. 13 to v. 27	" 15 to v. 36
24	" 47, v. 27, and 48	" 15, v. 21	" 49	" 15, v. 36, to 16, v. 16
25	" 50	" 16 to v. 24	Exodus 1	" 16, v. 16
26	Exodus 2	" 16, v. 24, to 17, v. 14	" 3	" 17 to v. 16
27	" 4 to v. 24	" 17, v. 14	" 4, v. 27, & 5 to 6, v. 2	" 17, v. 16
28	" 6, v. 2 to 14	" 18 to v. 21	" 6, v. 28, and 7	" 18 to v. 24
29	" 8, v. 1 to 20	" 18, v. 21, to 19, v. 3	" 8, v. 20, to 9, v. 13	" 18, v. 24, to 19, v. 21
30	" 9, v. 13	" 19, v. 3 to v. 27	" 10 to v. 21	" 19, v. 21
31	" 10, v. 21, and 11	" 19, v. 27, to 20, v. 17	" 12 to v. 21	" 20 to v. 17

TABLE OF DAILY LESSONS.—February hath 28 Days; but in every Leap-Year 29 Days.

	Morning.		Evening.	
	First Lesson.	Second Lesson.	First Lesson.	Second Lesson.
1	Exodus 12, v. 21 to v. 43	Matthew 20, v. 17	Exodus 12, v. 43, to 13, v. 17	Acts 20, v. 17
2	" 13, v. 17, to 14, v. 10	" 21 to v. 23	" 14, v. 10	" 21 to v. 17
3	" 15 to v. 22	" 21, v. 23	" 15, v. 22, to 16, v. 11	" 21, v. 17 to v. 37
4	" 16, v. 11	" 22 to v. 15	" 17	" 21, v. 37, to 22, v. 30
5	" 18	" 22, v. 15 to v. 41	" 19	" 22, v. 30, to 23, v. 12
6	" 20 to v. 22	" 22, v. 41, to 23, v. 13	" 21 to v. 18	" 23, v. 12
7	" 22, v. 21, to 23, v. 10	" 23, v. 13	" 23, v. 10	" 24
8	" 24	" 24 to v. 29	" 25 to v. 23	" 25
9	" 25, v. 23	" 24, v. 29	" 26 to v. 31	" 26
10	" 26, v. 31, and 27	" 25 to v. 31	" 28 to v. 39	" 27 to v. 18
11	" 29 to v. 38	" 25, v. 31	" 29, v. 38, to 30, v. 11	" 27, v. 18
12	" 30, v. 11	" 26 to v. 31	" 31	" 28 to v. 17
13	" 32 to v. 30	" 26, v. 31 to 57	" 32, v. 30, and 33	" 28, v. 17
14	" 34	" 26, v. 57	" 35 to v. 30	Rom. 1 to v. 18
15	" 35, v. 30, to 36, v. 8	" 27 to v. 27	" 39, v. 32	" 1, v. 18
16	" 40 to v. 17	" 27, v. 27 to v. 57	" 40, v. 17	" 2 to v. 17
17	Levit. 1	" 27, v. 57, and 28	Levit. 2	" 2, v. 17
18	" 3 to 6, v. 8	Mark 1 to v. 21	" 4	" 3
19	" 5 to 6, v. 8	" 1, v. 21	" 6, v. 8	" 4
20	" 7 to v. 28	" 2 to v. 23	" 7, v. 28, to 8, v. 13	" 5
21	" 8, v. 13	" 2, v. 23, to 3, v. 13	" 9 to v. 22	" 6
22	" 9, v. 22, and 10	" 3, v. 13	" 14 to v. 33	" 7
23	" 16	" 4 to v. 21	" 17 to v. 13	" 8 to v. 18
24	" 19 to v. 19	" 4, v. 21 to v. 35	" 19, v. 30, to 20, v. 9	" 8, v. 18
25	" 23 to v. 21	" 4, v. 35, to 5, v. 21	" 23, v. 21	" 9 to v. 19
26	" 24 to v. 17	" 5, v. 21	" 25 to v. 18	" 9, v. 19
27	" 25, v. 18 to v. 44	" 6 to v. 14	" 26 to v. 21	" 10
28	" 26, v. 21	" 6, v. 14 to v. 30	" 27	" 11 to v. 25
29	Num. 1, v. 47, to 2, v. 18	" 6, v. 30	" 3 to v. 14	" 11, v. 25 and 12

TABLE OF DAILY LESSONS.—MARCH hath 31 Days.

	MORNING.		EVENING.	
	First Lesson.	Second Lesson.	First Lesson.	Second Lesson.
1	Numbers 4, v. 46, to 5, v. 11	Mark 7 to v. 24	Numbers 6	Rom 13
2	„ 9, v. 15, to 10, v. 11	„ 7, v. 24, to 8, v. 10	„ 10, v. 11	„ 14 to 15, v. 8
3	„ 11 to v. 24	„ 8, v. 10, to 9, v. 2	„ 11, v. 24	„ 15, v. 8
4	„ 12	„ 9, v. 2 to v. 30	„ 13	„ 16
5	„ 14 to v. 26	„ 9, v. 30	„ 14, v. 26	1 Cor. 1 to v. 26
6	„ 16 to v. 23	„ 10 to v. 32	„ 16, v. 23	„ 1, v. 26, and 2
7	„ 17 and 18 to v. 28	„ 10, v. 32	„ 20	„ 3
8	„ 21	„ 11 to v. 27	„ 22 to v. 36	„ 4 to v. 18
9	„ 22, v. 36, and 23	„ 11, v. 27, to 12, v. 13	„ 24	„ 4, v. 18, and 5
10	„ 25	„ 12, v. 13 to v. 35	„ 27	„ 6
11	„ 33, v. 50, to 34, v. 16	„ 12, v. 35, to 13, v. 14	„ 35, v. 9 to v. 34	„ 7 to v. 25
12	Deut. 1 to v. 19	„ 13, v. 14	Deut. 1, v. 9	„ 7, v. 5
13	„ 2	„ 14 to v. 27	„ 3	„ 8
14	„ 4 to v. 25	„ 14, v. 27 to v. 53	„ 4, v. 25 to v. 41	„ 9 to v. 24
15	„ 5	„ 14, v. 53	„ 6	„ 9, v. 24, & 10 to v. 11, v. 2
16	„ 7	„ 15 to v. 42	„ 8	„ 11, v. 2
17	„ 9 to 10, v. 11	„ 15, v. 42, and 16	„ 10, v. 11, to 11, v. 18	„ 12 to v. 28
18	„ 11, v. 18	Luke 1 to v. 26	„ 12	„ 12, v. 28, and 13
19	„ 13	„ 1, v. 26 to v. 57	„ 14, v. 22, to 15, v. 16	„ 14 to v. 20
20	„ 16 to v. 18	„ 1, v. 57	„ 17, v. 8	„ 14, v. 20
21	„ 18	„ 2 to v. 21	„ 20	„ 15 to v. 35
22	„ 21, v. 22, to 22 v. 8	„ 2, v. 21 to v. 39	„ 24, v. 8	„ 15, v. 35
23	„ 26	„ 2, v. 39	„ 27	„ 16
24	„ 28 to v. 15	„ 3 to v. 23	„ 28, v. 15 to v. 47	2 Cor. 1 to v. 23
25	„ 28, v. 47, to 29, v. 2	„ 4 to v. 31	„ 29, v. 2	„ 1, v. 23, to 2, v. 14
26	„ 30	„ 4, v. 31, to 5, v. 12	„ 31	„ 2, v. 14, and 3
27	„ 32 to v. 44	„ 5, v. 12	„ 32, v. 44, and 33	„ 4
28	„ 34	„ 6, to v. 20	Joshua 1	„ 5
29	Joshua 2	„ 6, v. 20	„ 3	„ 6 to 7, v. 2
30	„ 4	„ 7 to v. 24	„ 5, v. 13, and 6	„ 7, v. 2
31	„ 7	„ 7, v. 24	„ 8 to v. 30	„ 8

TABLE OF DAILY LESSONS.—APRIL hath 30 Days.

	MORNING.		EVENING.	
	First Lesson.	Second Lesson.	First Lesson.	Second Lesson.
1	Joshua 9	Luke 8 to v. 26	Joshua 10 to v. 16	2 Cor. 9
2	" 14	" 8, v. 26	" 15 to v. 20	" 10
3	" 18 to v. 11	" 9 to v. 28	" 21, v. 43, to 22, v. 11	" 11 to v. 30
4	" 22, v. 11	" 9, v. 28 to v. 51	" 23	" 11, v. 30, to 12, v. 14
5	" 24	" 9, v. 51, to 10, v. 17	" 2	" 12, v. 14, and 13
6	Judges 3 to v. 12	" 10, v. 17	Judges 4	Gal. 1
7	" 5, v. 24	" 11 to v. 29	" 6 to v. 24	" 2
8	" 6, v. 32, to 9, v. 25	" 11, v. 29	" 7	" 3
9	" 8, v. 32, to 9, v. 25	" 12 to v. 35	" 10	" 4 to v. 21
10	" 11 to v. 29	" 12, v. 35	" 11, v. 29, to 12, v. 8	" 4, v. 21, to 5, v. 13
11	" 13	" 13 to v. 18	" 14	" 5, v. 13
12	" 15	" 13, v. 18	" 16	" 6
13	Ruth 1	" 14 to v. 25	Ruth 2	Eph. 1 to v. 15
14	" 3	" 14, v. 25, to 15, v. 11	" 4	" 1, v. 15, to 2, v. 11
15	1 Samuel 1	" 15, v. 11	1 Samuel 2 to v. 21	" 2, v. 11
16	" 2, v. 21	" 16	" 3	" 3
17	" 4	" 17 to v. 20	" 5	" 4 to v. 17
18	" 6 to 7, v. 2	" 17, v. 20	" 7, v. 2 to v. 17	" 4, v. 17, to 5, v. 15
19	" 8	" 18 to v. 31	" 9	" 5, v. 15, to 6, v. 10
20	" 10	" 18, v. 31, to 19, v. 11	" 11	" 6, v. 10
21	" 12	" 19, v. 11, to v. 28	" 13	Philip. 1
22	" 14 to v. 24	" 19, v. 28	" 14, v. 24	" 2
23	" 15	" 20 to v. 27	" 16	" 3 to 4, v. 2
24	" 17 to v. 31	" 20, v. 27, to 21, v. 5	" 17, v. 31 to v. 55	" 4, v. 2
25	" 17, v. 55, to 18, v. 17	" 21, v. 5	" 19	Colos. 1 to v. 21
26	" 20 to v. 18	" 22 to v. 31	" 20, v. 18	" 1, v. 21, to 2, v. 8
27	" 21 to 22, v. 6	" 22, v. 31 to v. 54	" 22, v. 6	" 2, v. 8
28	" 23	" 22, v. 54, to 23, v. 26	" 24 to 25, v. 2	" 3 to v. 18
29	" 26	" 23, v. 26 to v. 50	" 28, v. 3	" 3, v. 18, to 4, v. 27
30	" 29, v. 11, to 30, v. 26	" 23, v. 50, to 24, v. 13	" 31	" 4, v. 7

TABLE OF DAILY LESSONS.—May hath 31 Days.

	Morning.		Evening.	
	First Lesson.	Second Lesson.	First Lesson.	Second Lesson.
1	2 Samuel 1	Luke 24, v. 13 to v. 44	2 Samuel 3, v. 17	1 Thess. 1
2	" 4	" 24, v. 44	" 6	" 2
3	" 7	John 1 to v. 29	" 9, v. 13	" 3
4	" 11	" 1, v. 29	" 12 to v. 24	" 4
5	" 13, v. 38, to 14, v. 26	" 2	" 15 to v. 32	" 5
6	" 15, v. 32, to 16, v. 15	" 3 to v. 22	" 16, v. 15, to 17, v. 24	2 Thess. 2
7	" 17, v. 24, to 18, v. 18	" 3, v. 22	" 18, v. 18, to 19, v. 9	" 2
8	" 19, v. 9 to v. 24	" 4 to v. 31	" 19, v. 24	" 3
9	" 21 to v. 15	" 4, v. 31	" 23 to v. 24	1 Tim. 1 to v. 18
10	" 24	" 5 to v. 24	1 Kings 1 to v. 28	" 1, v. 18, and 2
11	1 Kings 1, v. 28	" 5, v. 24	" 3	" 3
12	" 4, v. 20	" 6 to v. 22	" 5	" 4
13	" 6	" 6, v. 22 to v. 41	" 7	" 5 to 6, v. 3
14	" 8 to v. 22	" 6, v. 41	" 8, v. 22 to v. 54	" 6, v. 3
15	" 8, v. 54, to 9, v. 10	" 7 to v. 25	" 10	2 Tim. 1
16	" 11 to v. 26	" 7, v. 25	" 11, v. 26	" 2
17	" 12 to v. 25	" 8 to v. 31	" 12, v. 25, to 13, v. 11	" 3
18	" 13, v. 11	" 8, v. 31	" 14 to v. 21	" 4
19	" 15 to v. 25	" 9 to v. 39	" 15, v. 25, to 16, v. 8	Titus 1
20	" 16, v. 8	" 9, v. 39, to 10, v. 22	" 17	" 2
21	" 18 to v. 17	" 10, v. 22	" 18, v. 17	" 3
22	" 19	" 11 to v. 47	" 20 to v. 27	Philemon
23	" 20, v. 27	" 11, v. 47, to 12, v. 20	" 21	Hebrews 1 to 2, v. 5.
24	" 22 to v. 41	" 12, v. 20	2 Kings 1	" 2, v. 5, to 3, v. 7
25	2 Kings 2	" 13, v. 21	" 3	" 3, v. 7, to 4, v. 14
26	" 4	" 14	" 5	" 4, v. 14, and 5
27	" 6	" 15	" 7	" 6
28	" 8 to v. 16	" 16 to v. 16	" 9	" 7
29	" 10 to v. 18	" 16, v. 16	" 10, v. 18	" 8
30	" 12	" 17	" 13	" 9
31	" 14		" 16	" 10 to v. 19

TABLE OF DAILY LESSONS.—JUNE hath 30 Days.

	MORNING		EVENING	
	First Lesson.	Second Lesson	First Lesson.	Second Lesson.
1	2 Kings 17 to v. 24	John 18 to v. 28	2 Kings 17, v. 24	Hebrews 10, v. 19
2	" 18	" 18, v. 28, to 19, v. 17	" 19 to v. 20	" 11 to v. 17
3	" 19, v. 20	" 19, v. 17	" 20	" 11, v. 17
4	" 21	" 20	" 22	" 12
5	" 23 to v. 24	" 21	" 23, v. 24, to 24, v. 8	" 13
6	" 24, v. 8, to 25, v. 8	Acts 1	" 25, v. 8	James 1
7	1 Chron. 13	" 2 to v. 22	1 Chron. 15 to 16, v. 4	" 2
8	" 16, v. 4	" 2, v. 22	" 17	" 3
9	" 21 to 22, v. 2	" 3	" 22, v. 2, to 23, v. 2	" 4
10	" 28	" 4 to v. 32	" 29	" 5
11	2 Chron. 1	" 4, v. 32, to 5, v. 17	2 Chron. 12	1 Peter 1 to v. 22
12	" 13	" 5, v. 17	" 14	" 1, v. 22, to 2, v. 11
13	" 15	" 6	" 16	" 2, v. 11, to 3, v. 8
14	" 17 to v. 14	" 7 to v. 35	" 19	" 3, v. 8, to 4, v. 7
15	" 20 to 21, v. 2	" 7, v. 35, to 8, v. 5	" 21, v. 2	" 4, v. 7
16	" 22	" 8, v. 5 to v. 26	" 23	" 5
17	" 24	" 8, v. 26	" 25	2 Peter 1
18	" 26 and 27	" 9 to v. 23	" 28	" 2
19	" 29 to v. 21	" 9, v. 23	" 29, v. 21	" 3
20	" 30 to 31, v. 2	" 10 to v. 24	" 31, v. 2	1 John 1
21	" 32	" 10, v. 24	" 33	" 2 to v. 15
22	" 34	" 11 to v. 27	" 35	" 2, v. 15
23	" 36	" 11, v. 27, and 12	Ezra 1 and 3	" 3 to v. 16
24	Ezra 4	" 13 to v. 14	" 5	" 3, v. 16, to 4, v. 7
25	" 6	" 13, v. 14 to v. 44	" 7	" 4, v. 7
26	" 8, v. 15	" 13, v. 44, to 14, v. 8	" 9	" 5
27	" 10 to v. 20	" 14, v. 8	Neh. 1	
28	Neh. 2	" 15 to v. 36	" 4	2 John
29	" 5	" 15, v. 36, to 16, v. 16	" 6 to 7, v. 5	3 John
30	" 7, v. 73, and 8	" 16, v. 16	" 9	Jude Revelation 1

TABLE OF DAILY LESSONS.—July hath 31 Days.

	MORNING		EVENING	
	First Lesson.	Second Lesson.	First Lesson.	Second Lesson.
1	Nehemiah 10, v. 28 to v. 39	Acts 17 to v. 16	Nehemiah 12, v. 44, to 13, v. 15	Revelation 2 to v. 18
2	" 13, v. 15	" 17, v. 16	Esther 1	" 2, v. 18, to 3, v. 7
3	Esther 2, v. 15, and 3	" 18 to v. 24	" 4 to 5, v. 9	" 3, v. 7
4	" 5, v. 9, to 6, v. 14	" 18, v. 24, to 19, v. 21	" 6, v. 14, & 7 to 8, v. 3	" 4
5	" 8, v. 3	" 19, v. 21	" 9 and 10	" 5
6	Job 1	" 20 to v. 17	Job 2	" 6
7	" 3	" 20, v. 17	" 4	" 7 to 8, v. 2
8	" 5	" 21 v. 17	" 6	" 8, v. 2 to v. 13
9	" 7	" 21, v. 17 to v. 37	" 8	" 8, v. 13, to 9, v. 12
10	" 9	" 21, v. 37, to 22, v. 30	" 10	" 9, v. 12
11	" 11	" 22, v. 30, to 23, v. 12	" 12	" 10
12	" 13	" 23, v. 12	" 14	" 11
13	" 15 to v. 14, and 16	" 24	" 17	" 12
14	" 18	" 25	" 19	" 13
15	" 20	" 26	" 21	" 14
16	" 22	" 27 to v. 18	" 23	" 15
17	" 24	" 27, v. 18	" 25 and 26	" 16
18	" 27	" 28 to v. 17	" 28	" 17
19	" 29 to 30, v. 2	" 28, v. 17	" 30, v. 12 to v. 27	" 18
20	" 31, v. 13, to 32, v. 2	Romans 1 to v. 18	" 32, v. 2	" 19 to v. 11
21	" 33	" 1, v. 18	" 34	" 19, v. 11
22	" 36	" 2 to v. 17	" 38 to v. 39	" 20
23	" 38, v. 39, and 39	" 2, v. 17	" 40	" 21 to v. 15
24	" 41	" 3	" 42	" 21, v. 15, to 22, v. 6
25	Proverbs 1 to v. 20	" 4	Proverbs 1, v. 20	" 22, v. 6
26	" 2	" 5	" 3	Matthew 1
27	" 4	" 6	" 5	" 2
28	" 6 to v. 20	" 7	" 7	" 3
29	" 8	" 8 to v. 18	" 9	" 4 to v. 23
30	" 10, to or from v. 16	" 8, v. 18	" 11, to or from v. 15	" 4, v. 23, to 5, v. 13
31	" 12	" 9 to v. 19	" 13	" 5, v. 13 to v. 27

TABLE OF DAILY LESSONS.—August hath 31 Days.

	Morning		Evening	
	First Lesson.	Second Lesson.	First Lesson.	Second Lesson.
1	Proverbs 14 to v. 18	Romans 9, v. 19	Proverbs 14, v. 18	Matthew 5, v. 27, to 6, v. 19
2	" 15 to v. 19	" 10	" 15, v. 19	" 6, v. 10
3	" 16	" 11 to v. 25	" 17 to v. 15	" 7
4	" 17, v. 15	" 11, v. 25	" 18	" 8 to v. 18
5	" 19	" 12	" 20 to v. 23	" 8, v. 18
6	" 21 to v. 17	" 13	" 21, v. 17	" 9 to v. 18
7	" 22 to v. 17	" 14 to 15, v. 8	" 22, v. 17	" 9, v. 18
8	" 23, v. 10	" 15, v. 8	" 24	" 10 to v. 24
9	" 25	" 16	" 26	" 10, v. 24, to 11, v. 2
10	" 27 to v. 23	1 Cor. 1 to v. 26	" 28 to v. 14	" 11, v. 2
11	" 28, v. 14	" 1, v. 26, and 2	" 29	" 12 to v. 22
12	" 30 to v. 18	" 3	" 31, v. 10	" 12, v. 22
13	Eccles. 1	" 4 to v. 18	Eccles. 2 to v. 24	" 13 to v. 24
14	" 2, v. 24, to 3, v. 16	" 4, v. 18, and 5	" 3, v. 16, and 4	" 13, v. 24 to v. 53
15	" 5	" 6	" 6	" 13, v. 53, to 14, v. 13
16	" 7	" 7 to v. 25	" 8	" 14, v. 13
17	" 9	" 7, v. 25	" 10	" 15 to v. 21
18	" 11	" 8	" 12	" 15, v. 21
19	S. of Sol. 2	" 9 to v. 24	S. of Sol. 3 to v. 8, and v. 14	" 16 to v. 24
20	" 4, v. 16, to 5, v. 9	" 9, v. 24, & 10 to 11, v. 2	Isaiah 2	" 16, v. 24, to 17, v. 14
21	Isaiah 1	" 11, v. 2 to v. 17	" 4, v. 2	" 17, v. 14
22	" 3	" 11, v. 17	" 5, v. 18	" 18 to v. 21
23	" 5 to v. 18	" 12 to v. 28	" 7 to v. 17	" 18, v. 21, to 19, v. 3
24	" 6	" 12, v. 28, and 13	" 8, v. 18, to 9, v. 8	" 19, v. 3 to v. 27
25	" 8, v. 5 to v. 18	" 14 to v. 20	" 10, v. 5 to v. 20	" 19, v. 27, to 20, v. 17
26	" 9, v. 8, to 10, v. 5	" 14, v. 20	" 11	" 20, v. 17
27	" 10, v. 20	" 15 to v. 35	" 13	" 21 to v. 23
28	" 12	" 15, v. 35	" 14, v. 24 to v. 32	" 21, v. 23
29	" 14 to v. 24	" 16	" 18	" 22 to v. 15
30	" 17	2 Cor. 1 to v. 23	" 19, v. 16	" 22, v. 15 to v. 41
31	" 19 to v. 16	" 1, v. 23, to 2, v. 14		" 22, v. 41, to 23, v. 13

TABLE OF DAILY LESSONS.—SEPTEMBER hath 30 Days.

	MORNING.			EVENING.	
	First Lesson.	Second Lesson.		First Lesson.	Second Lesson.
1	Isaiah 21 to v. 13	2 Cor. 2, v. 14, and 3	Isaiah	22 to v. 15	Matthew 23, v. 13
2	" 22, v. 15	" 4	"	23	" 24 to v. 29
3	" 24	" 5	"	25	" 24. v. 29
4	" 26 to v. 20	" 6 to 7, v. 2	"	26, v. 20, and 27	" 25 to v. 31
5	" 28 to v. 14	" 7, v. 2	"	28, v. 14	" 25, v. 31
6	" 29	" 8	"	30 to v. 18	" 26 to v. 31
7	" 30, v. 18	" 9	"	31	" 26, v. 31 to v. 57
8	" 32	" 10	"	33	" 26, v. 57
9	" 34	" 11 to v. 30	"	35	" 27 to v. 27
10	" 36 to v. 22	" 11, v. 30, to 12, v. 14	"	36, v. 22, to 37, v. 20	" 27, v. 27 to v. 57
11	" 37, v. 20	" 12, v. 14, and 13	"	38	" 27, v. 57, and 28
12	" 39	Galatians 1	"	40	Mark 1 to v. 21
13	" 41 to v. 17	" 2	"	41, v. 17	" 1, v. 21
14	" 42 to v. 18	" 3	"	42, v. 18, to 43, v. 8	" 2 to v. 23
15	" 43, v. 8 to v. 28	" 4 to v. 21	"	44 to v. 21	" 2, v. 23, to 3, v. 13
16	" 44, v. 21, to 45, v. 9	" 4, v. 21, to 5, v. 13	"	45, v. 9	" 3, v. 13
17	" 46	" 5, v. 13	"	47	" 4 to v. 21
18	" 48	" 6	"	49 to v. 13	" 4, v. 21 to v. 35
19	" 49, v. 13	Eph. 1 to v. 15	"	50	" 4, v. 35, to 5, v. 21
20	" 51	" 1, v. 15, to 2, v. 11	"	52 to v. 13	" 5, v. 21.
21	" 52, v. 13, and 53	" 2, v. 11	"	54	" 6 to v. 14
22	" 55	" 3 to v. 17	"	56	" 6, v. 14 to v. 30
23	" 57	" 4, v. 17, to 5, v. 15	"	58	" 6, v. 30
24	" 59	" 5, v. 15, to 6, v. 10	"	60	" 7 to v. 24
25	" 61	" 6, v. 10	"	62	" 7, v. 24, to 8, v. 10
26	" 63, v. 8	Philip. 1	"	64 to 65, v. 8	" 8, v. 10, to 9, v. 2
27	" 65, v. 15	" 2	"	66 to v. 15	" 9, v. 2 to v. 30
28	" 66, v. 15	" 3 to 4, v. 2	Jeremiah 1		" 9, v. 30
29	Jeremiah 2 to v. 20	" 4, v. 2.	"	3, v. 12 to v. 25	" 10 to v. 32
30	" 4, v. 5 to v. 19		"	4, v. 21	" 10, v. 32

TABLE OF DAILY LESSONS.—October hath 31 Days.

	MORNING.		EVENING.	
	First Lesson.	Second Lesson.	First Lesson.	Second Lesson.
1	Jeremiah 5 to v. 19	Colossians 1 to v. 21	Jeremiah 5, v. 19	Mark 11 to v. 27
2	6 to v. 22	1, v. 21 to 2, v. 8	7 to v. 17	11, v. 27, to 12, v. 13
3	7, v. 17	2, v. 8	8 to 9, v. 2	12, v. 13 to v. 35
4	9, v. 2 to v. 25	3 to v. 18	10 to v. 17	12, v. 35, to 13, v. 14
5	10, v. 17	3, v. 18, to 4, v. 7	11 to v. 14	13, v. 14
6	12	4, v. 7	13, v. 8 to v. 24	14 to v. 27
7	14, v. 7	1 Thess. 1	15	14, v. 27 to v. 53
8	16	" 2	17 to v. 19	14, v. 53
9	17, v. 19	" 3	18 to v. 18	15 to v. 42
10	19	" 4	20 to v. 14	15, v. 42, and 16
11	21	" 5	22 to v. 13	Luke 1 to v. 26
12	22, v. 13	2 Thess. 1	23 to v. 16	1, v. 26 to v. 57
13	23, v. 16 to v. 33	" 2	24	1, v. 57
14	25 to v. 15	" 3	25, v. 30	2 to v. 21
15	26	1 Timothy 1 to v. 18	27	2, v. 21 to v. 39
16	27	1, v. 18, and 2	29, v. 4 to v. 20	2, v. 39
17	30	" 3	31 to v. 15	3 to v. 23
18	31, v. 15 to v. 38	" 4	32 to v. 26	4 to v. 31
19	32, v. 26	" 5 to 6, v. 3	33 to v. 14	4, v. 31, to 5, v. 12.
20	33, v. 14	" 6, v. 3	34, v. 8	5, v. 12
21	35	2 Timothy 1	36 to v. 14	6 to v. 20
22	36, v. 14	" 2	37 to 38, v. 7	6, v. 20
23	38, v. 7	" 3	39	7 to v. 24
24	40 to 41, v. 4	" 4	41, v. 16, to 42, v. 19	7, v. 24
25	42, v. 19, to 43, v. 8	Titus 1	43, v. 8, to 44, v. 15	8 to v. 26
26	44, v. 15	" 2	45 to 46, v. 11	8, v. 26
27	46, v. 13	" 3	47	9 to v. 28
28	48 to v. 14	Philemon	49, v. 20 to v. 39	9, v. 28 to v. 51
29	50 to v. 21	Hebrews 1 to 2, v. 5	50, v. 21	9, v. 51, to 10, v. 17
30	51 v. 11	" 2, v. 5, to 3, v. 7	51, v. 13 to v. 27	10, v. 17
31	51, v. 27 to v. 41	" 3, v. 7, to 4, v. 14.	51, v. 41 to v. 54	11 to v. 29

TABLE OF DAILY LESSONS.—NOVEMBER hath 30 Days.

	Morning.		Evening.	
	First Lesson.	Second Lesson.	First Lesson.	Second Lesson.
1	Jer. 51, v. 54	Hebrews 4, v. 14, and 5	Lam. 1 to v. 15	Luke 11, v. 29
2	Lam. 2	" 6	" 3 to v. 34	" 12 to v. 35
3	" 3, v. 34	" 7	Ezekiel 2 and 3 to v. 15	" 13 to v. 18
4	Ezek. 1	" 8	" 5, v. 5	" 13, v. 18
5	" 3, v. 15	" 9	" 9	" 14 to v. 25
6	" 8	" 10 to v. 19	" 11	" 14, v. 25, to 15, v. 11
7	" 10	" 10, v. 19	" 13 to v. 17	" 15, v. 11
8	" 12	" 11 to v. 17	" 15	" 16
9	" 14	" 11, v. 17	" 17	" 17 to v. 20
10	" 16, v. 44	" 12	" 19, v. 10, to 20, v. 18	" 17, v. 20
11	" 18	" 13	" 21	" 18 to v. 31
12	" 20, v. 18	James 1	" 24, v. 15	" 18, v. 31, to 19, v. 11
13	" 22 to v. 5, & v. 17 to v. 31	" 2	" 27	" 19, v. 11 to v. 28
14	" 26	" 3	" 31	" 19, v. 28
15	" 28	" 4	" 33 to v. 21	" 20 to v. 27
16	" 32 to v. 17	" 5	" 34	" 20, v. 27, to 21, v. 5
17	" 33, v. 21	1 Peter 1 to v. 22	" 36, v. 16	" 21, v. 5
18	" 36 to v. 16	" 1, v. 22, to 2, v. 11	" 38, v. 14	" 22 to v. 51
19	" 37	" 2, v. 11, to 3, v. 8	" 40 to v. 28	" 22, v. 31 to v. 54
20	" 39, v. 21	" 3, v. 8, to 4, v. 7	" 41	" 22, v. 54, to 23, v. 26
21	" 40, v. 28	" 4, v. 7	" 43 to 44, v. 4	" 23, v. 26 to v. 50
22	" 42	" 5	" 45	" 23, v. 50, to 24, v. 13
23	" 44, v. 4	2 Peter 1	" 47 to v. 13	" 24, v. 13 to v. 44
24	" 46	" 2	Daniel 1	" 24, v. 44
25	" 48	" 3	" 2, v. 24	John 1 to v. 29
26	Daniel 2 to v. 24	1 John 1	" 4	" 1, v. 29
27	" 3	" 2, v. 15	" 6	" 2
28	" 5	" 2, v. 15	" 8	" 3 to v. 22
29	" 7	" 3, v. 16	" 10 to v. 20	" 3, v. 22
30	" 9	" 3, v. 16, to 4, v. 7		

TABLE OF DAILY LESSONS.—DECEMBER hath 31 Days.

	Morning.		Evening.	
	First Lesson.	Second Lesson.	First Lesson.	Second Lesson.
1	Daniel 10, v. 20, to 11, v. 35	1 John 4, v. 7	Daniel 11, v. 35, and 12	John 4 to v. 31
2	Hosea 2, v. 14.	" 5	Hosea 3, v. 4, to 4, v. 13	" 4, v. 31
3	" 5, v. 8, to 6, v. 7	2 John	" 7, v. 8, and 8	" 5 to v. 24
4	" 9	3 John	" 10	" 5, v. 24
5	" 11 to 12, v. 7	Jude	" 13 to v. 15	" 6 to v. 22
6	" 14	Rev. 1	Joel 1	" 6, v. 22 to v. 41
7	Joel 2 to v. 28	" 2 to v. 18	" 2, v. 28, and 3	" 6, v. 41
8	Amos 1 to 2, v. 4	" 2, v. 18, to 3, v. 7	Amos 2, v. 4, to 3, v. 9	" 7 to v. 25
9	" 4, v. 4 to v. 13	" 3, v. 7	" 5 to v. 18	" 7, v. 25
10	" 5, v. 18, to 6, v. 9	" 4	" 7	" 8 to v. 31
11	" 8	" 5	" 9	" 8, v. 31
12	Book of Obadiah	" 6	Jonah 1 and 2	" 9 to v. 39
13	Jonah 3 and 4	" 7 to 8, v. 2	Micah 1 to v. 10	" 9, v. 39, to 10, v. 22
14	Micah 2	" 8, v. 2 to v. 13	" 3 to 4, v. 9	" 10, v. 22
15	" 4, v. 9, and 5	" 8, v. 13, to 9, v. 12	" 6	" 11 to v. 47
16	" 7	" 9, v. 12	Nahum 1 to v. 15	" 11, v. 47, to 12, v. 20
17	Nahum 1, v. 15, and 2	" 10	" 3	" 12, v. 20
18	Habak. 1	" 11	Habak. 2	" 13 to v. 21
19	" 3	" 12	Zeph. 1 to 2, v. 4	" 13, v. 21
20	Zeph. 2, v. 4	" 13	Haggai 2 to v. 10	" 14
21	Haggai 1	" 14	Zechariah 1 to v. 18	" 15
22	" 2, v. 10	" 15	" 3	" 16 to v. 16
23	Zechariah 1, v. 18, and 2	" 16	" 5	" 16, v. 16
24	" 4	" 17	" 7	" 17
25	" 6	" 18	" 9	" 18 to v. 28
26	" 8	" 19 to v. 11	" 11	" 18, v. 28
27	" 10	" 19, v. 11	" 13	" 19 to v. 25
28	" 12	" 20	Malachi 1	" 19, v. 25
29	Malachi 2 to v. 10	" 21 to v. 15	" 2, v. 10	" 20 to v. 19
30	" 3 to v. 13	" 21, v. 15 to 22, v. 6	" 3, v. 13, and 4	" 20, v. 19
31		" 22, v. 6		" 21

Table

of

Psalms for every Month

PSALMS FOR EVERY MONTH.

Day.	January. Morning.	January. Evening.	February. Morning.	February. Evening.	March. Morning.	March. Evening.	April. Morning.	April. Evening.
1	1, 2	3, 4	80	81, 82	1, 2	3, 4	80	81, 82
2	5, 6	7, 8	83	84	5, 6	7, 8	83	84
3	9	10	85	86, 87	9	10	85	86, 87
4	11, 12, 13	14, 15, 16	88	89 to v. 19	11, 12, 13	14, 15, 16	88	89 to v. 19
5	17	18 to v. 20	89, v. 19	90	18 to v. 20	89, v. 19	90
6	18, v. 20	19	91	92, 93	18, v. 20	19	91	92, 93
7	20, 21	22	94	95, 96	20, 21	22	94	95, 96
8	23, 24	25	97, 98	99, 100, 101	23, 24	25	97, 98	99, 100, 101
9	26, 27	28, 29	102	103	26, 27	28, 29	102	103
10	30	31	104	105	30	31	104	105
11	32	33	106 to v. 34	106, v. 34	32	33	106 to v. 34	106, v. 34
12	34	35	107 to v. 23	107, v. 23	34	35	107 to v. 23	107, v. 23
13	36	37 to v. 23	108	109	36	37 to v. 23	108	109
14	37, v. 23	38	110, 111, 112	113, 114	37, v. 23	38	110, 111, 112	113, 114
15	39	40	115	116, 117	39	40	115	116, 117
16	41	42, 43	118	119 to v. 17	41	42, 43	118	119 to v. 17
17	44	45	119, v. 25 to v. 57	119, v. 57 to v. 81	44	45	119, v. 17 to v. 33	119, v. 33 to v. 49
18	46, 47	48	119, v. 81 to v. 97	119, v. 97 to v. 113	46, 47	48	119, v. 49 to v. 65	119, v. 65 to v. 81
19	49	50	119, v. 113 to v. 129	119, v. 129 to v. 145	49	50	119, v. 81 to v. 97	119, v. 97 to v. 113
20	51	52, 53, 54	119, v. 145 to v. 161	119, v. 161	51	52, 53, 54	119, v. 113 to v. 129	119, v. 129 to v. 145
21	55	56	120, 121, 122	123, 124, 125	55	56	119, v. 145 to v. 161	119, v. 161
22	57, 58	59	126, 127, 128	129, 130, 131	57, 58	59	120, 121, 122	123, 124, 125
23	60, 61	62, 63	132, 133	134, 135	60, 61	62, 63	126, 127, 128	129, 130, 131
24	64, 65	66	136	137, 138	64, 65	66	132, 133	134, 135
25	67, 68 to v. 17	68, v. 17	139	140	67, 68 to v. 17	68, v. 17	136	137, 138
26	69 to v. 20	69, v. 20, 70	141, 142	143	69 to v. 20	69, v. 20, & 70	139	140
27	71	72	144	145	71	72	141, 142	143
28	73	74	146	147	73	74	144	145
29	75, 76	77	148	149, 150	75, 76	77	146	147
30	78 to v. 32	78, v. 32 to v. 55			78 to v. 32	78, v. 32 to v. 55	148	149, 150

PSALMS FOR EVERY MONTH.

Day.	MAY. Morning.	MAY. Evening.	JUNE. Morning.	JUNE. Evening.	JULY. Morning.	JULY. Evening.	AUGUST. Morning.	AUGUST. Evening.
1	1, 2	3, 4	..	81, 82	1, 2	3, 4	80	81, 82
2	5, 6	7, 8	..	84	5, 6	7, 8	83	84
3	9	10	..	86, 87	9	10	85	86, 87
4	11, 12, 13	14, 15, 16	89, v. 19	89 v. 19	11, 12, 13	14, 15, 16	88	89 to v. 19
5	17	18 to v. 20	..	90	17	18 to v. 20	89, v. 19	90
6	18, v. 20	19	91	92, 93	18, v. 20	19	91	92, 93
7	20, 21	22	94	95, 96	20, 21	22	94	95, 96
8	23, 24	25	97, 98	99, 100, 101	23, 24	25	97, 98	99, 100, 101
9	26, 27	28, 29	102	103	26, 27	28, 29	102	103
10	30	31	104	104, v. 24	30	31	104 to v. 24	104, v. 24
11	32	33	105	105, v. 23	32	33	105	105, v. 23
12	34	35	106 to v. 34	106, v. 34	34	35	106 to v. 34	106, v. 34
13	36	37 to v. 23	107 v. 23	107, v. 23	36	37 to v. 23	107 to v. 23	107, v. 23
14	37, v. 23	38	108	109	37, v. 23	38	108	109
15	39	40	110, 111, 112	113, 114	39	40	110, 111, 112	113, 114
16	41	42, 43	115	116, 117	41	42, 43	115	116, 117
17	44	45	118	119 to v. 17	44	45	118	119 to v. 17
18	46, 47	48	119, v. 17 to v. 33	119, v. 33 to v. 49	46, 47	48	119, v. 17 to v. 33	119, v. 33 to v. 49
19	49	50	119, v. 49 to v. 65	119, v. 65 to v. 81	49	50	119, v. 49 to v. 65	119, v. 65 to v. 81
20	51	52, 53, 54	119, v. 81 to v. 97	119, v. 97 to v. 113	51	52, 53, 54	119, v. 81 to v. 97	119, v. 97 to v. 113
21	55	56	119, v. 113 to v. 129	119, v. 129 to v. 145	55	56	119, v. 113 to v. 129	119, v. 129 to v. 145
22	57, 58	59	119, v. 145 to v. 161	119, v. 161	57, 58	59	119, v. 145 to v. 161	119, v. 161
23	60, 61	62, 63	120, 121, 122	123, 124, 125	60, 61	62, 63	120, 121, 122	123, 124, 125
24	64, 65	66	126, 127, 128	129, 130, 131	64, 65	66	126, 127, 128	129, 130, 131
25	67, 68 to v. 17	68, v. 17	132, 133	134, 135	67, 68 to v. 17	68, v. 17	132, 133	134, 135
26	69 to v. 20	69, v. 20, & 70	136	137, 138	69 to v. 20	69, v. 20, & 70	136	137, 138
27	71	72	139	140	71	72	139	140
28	73	74	141, 142	143	73	74	141, 142	143
29	75, 76	77	144	145	75, 76	77	144	145
30	78 to v. 32	78, v. 32 to v. 55	146	147	78 to v. 32	78, v. 32 to v. 55	146	147
31	78, v. 55	79	148	..	78, v. 55	79	148	149, 150

PSALMS FOR EVERY MONTH.

Day.	September Morning.	September Evening.	October Morning.	October Evening.	November Morning.	November Evening.	December Morning.	December Evening.
1	1, 2	3, 4	78, v. 55	79	1, 2	3, 4	78, v. 55	79
2	5, 6	7, 8	80	81, 82	5, 6	7, 8	80	81, 82
3	9	10	83	84	9	10	83	84
4	11, 12, 13	14, 15, 16	85	86, 87	11, 12, 13	14, 15, 16	85	86, 87
5	17	18 to v. 20	88	89 to v. 19	17	18 to v. 20	88	89 to v. 19
6	18, v. 20	19	89, v. 19	90	18, v. 20	19	89, v. 19	90
7	20, 21	22	91	92, 93	20, 21	22	91	92, 93
8	23, 24	25	94	95, 96	23, 24	25	94	95, 96
9	26, 27	28, 29	97, 98	99, 100, 101	26, 27	28, 29	97, 98	99, 100, 101
10	30	31	102	103	30	31	102	103
11	32	33	104	105	32	33	104	105
12	34	35	106 to v. 34	106, v. 34	34	35	106 to v. 34	106, v. 34
13	36	37 to v. 23	107 to v. 23	107, v. 23	36	37 to v. 23	107 to v. 23	107, v. 23
14	37, v. 23	38	108	109	37, v. 23	38	108	109
15	39	40	110, 111, 112	113, 114	39	40	110, 111, 112	113, 114
16	41	42, 43	115	116, 117	41	42, 43	115	116, 117
17	44	45	118	119 to v. 17	44	45	118	119 to v. 17
18	46, 47	48	119, v. 17 to v. 33	119, v. 33 to v. 49	46, 47	48	119, v. 17 to v. 33	119, v. 33 to v. 49
19	49	50	119, v. 49 to v. 65	119, v. 65 to v. 81	49	50	119, v. 49 to v. 65	119, v. 65 to v. 81
20	51	52, 53, 54	119, v. 81 to v. 97	119, v. 97 to v. 113	51	52, 53, 54	119, v. 81 to v. 97	119, v. 97 to v. 113
21	55	56	119, v. 113 to v. 129	119, v. 129 to v. 145	55	56	119, v. 113 to v. 129	119, v. 129 to v. 145
22	57, 58	59	119, v. 145 to v. 161	119, v. 161	57, 58	59	119, v. 145 to v. 161	119, v. 161
23	60, 61	62, 63	120, 121, 122	123, 124, 125	60, 61	62, 63	120, 121, 122	123, 124, 125
24	64, 65	66	126, 127, 128	129, 130, 131	64, 65	66	126, 127, 128	129, 130, 131
25	67, 68 to v. 17	68, v. 17	132, 133	134, 135	67, 68 to v. 17	68, v. 17	132, 133	134, 135
26	69 to v. 20	69, v. 20, & 70	136	137, 138	69 to v. 20	69, v. 20, & 70	136	137, 138
27	71	72	139	140	71	72	139	140
28	73	74	141, 142	143	73	74	141, 142	143
29	75, 76	77	144	145	75, 76	77	144	145
30	78 to v. 32	78, v. 32 to v. 55	146	147	78 to v. 32	78, v. 32 to v. 55	146	147
31								149, 150

THE

ORDER OF DIVINE SERVICE.

First Sunday of the Month.

Morning Service.

(The Rubrics annexed to the First Morning Service apply, likewise, to the Services that follow for the five Sundays of the month.)

At the entry of the officiating Minister, one of the invitatory Psalms may be sung; then the Minister says—

OUR help is in the name of the Lord, who made heaven and earth.

The Lord is nigh unto all them that call upon Him, to all that call upon Him in truth. He will fulfil the desire of them that fear Him; He also will hear their cry, and will save them.

Having these promises, let us draw near to the throne of grace with true hearts, in full assurance of faith.

I.

Prayer of Invocation.

ALMIGHTY God, our heavenly Father, being now assembled to present to Thee our praises and our prayers, and to hear Thy word; we beseech Thee, that, according to the promises which Thou hast made to hear us when we call upon Thee in the name of Thy Son, it may please Thee to regard us in Thy mercy, and so to raise our thoughts and desires to Thyself, that we may this day render to Thee an acceptable service; through Jesus Christ our Lord.

The Confession.

If we say we have no sin, we deceive ourselves, and the truth is not in us. If we confess our sins, Thou art faithful and just to forgive us our sins, and to cleanse us from all unrighteousness.

O Lord our God, eternal and almighty Father, we acknowledge and confess before Thy holy majesty, that we are miserable sinners; born in iniquity, prone to evil; unable of ourselves to do that which is good; transgressing daily, and in many ways, Thy holy commandments, and by Thy just judgment deserving of condemnation and death. But, O Lord, we are deeply grieved for having offended Thee. We condemn both ourselves and our sins with unfeigned penitence. We seek refuge in Thy mercy, and humbly entreat Thee to help us in our misery.

Be pleased then, O most gracious God, Father of mercies, to have compassion on us, and for the sake of Jesus Christ Thy Son, to pardon all our sins. Grant unto us also, and increase in us from day to day, the grace of Thy Holy Spirit, that acknowledging and bewailing more and more our iniquities, we may renounce them with all our hearts, and may bring forth the fruits of holiness and righteousness, which are well-pleasing in Thy sight; through Jesus Christ our Lord.

For Pardon and Peace.

Blessed be Thy name, O Lord, that according to the comforting assurance of Thy grace promised in the Gospel, Thou dost forgive in heaven, the sins of all who truly repent, believe in the Lord Jesus Christ, and are resolved to walk in newness of life. Grant, we beseech Thee, to all such here present the full assurance of pardon and reconciliation, and the peace which passeth all understanding; through Jesus Christ our Lord.

Supplications.

Give ear, O Lord, unto our prayer, and attend to the voice of our supplication.

Save us from any dangers that may beset us. Deliver us from our sins; preserve us from every wicked thought, from pride, impiety, hypocrisy, and everything that is contrary to Thy will. Direct us always by Thy grace, O merciful God, and lead us continually by Thy Spirit. Give us at all times good and holy thoughts, pure, gentle, and peaceable dispositions, an entire resignation to Thy providence, an ardent love to Thee, and a sincere charity towards all mankind.

Wean our hearts from this vain world, and give us grace to have them always lifted up to heaven where our treasure is; so that watching and praying without ceasing, and living in temperance, righteousness, and piety, we may pass our days in peace, waiting for the glorious return of our Saviour; and that when He shall come to judge the world, we may appear before Thee without confusion, and without fear.

Almighty God, our Father and Preserver, who of Thy goodness hast watched over us during the past night, and brought us to this day, strengthen and guard us by Thy Spirit, we beseech Thee, that we may spend it wholly in

Thy service, seeking Thy glory, and the salvation of our fellow-men. And even as Thou sheddest now the beams of the sun upon the earth to give light unto our bodies, so do Thou illuminate our souls with the brightness of Thy Spirit, to guide us in the paths of holy obedience.

Here may be introduced any other subject for Supplication.

O God hear us; reject not the supplications of Thy servants, but grant us the good things we have asked of Thee, and all others which are necessary for us; through Jesus Christ our Lord: to whom with Thee the Father and the Holy Ghost, be the glory, as it was in the beginning, is now, and ever shall be, world without end.

Here, and at the end of all the other Prayers, the Congregation say AMEN.

Then are read the Lessons from the Old and New Testaments; and a portion of the Psalter may be read or sung. Before reading the Lessons may be said: "Hear, with reverence, the word of God, as it is written in the   chapter of the Book of   , at the   verse;" and at the end of the Lessons, " The Lord bless to us the reading of His Word, and to His name be the glory and praise. Amen." Then may be sung a Psalm or Hymn; after which the Minister says—

LET US PRAY.

II.

The Thanksgiving.

O LORD, open Thou our lips, and our mouth shall show forth Thy praise.

O God, Thy glory is great in all the Churches, and the praises of Thy name resound in the assemblies of Thy saints. We, Thy servants, would humble ourselves before Thee: we worship Thine infinite majesty; we celebrate Thy wisdom, power, and goodness, that shine forth in the works of creation and redemption, through Jesus Christ our Lord. We bless Thee for all temporal and spiritual good that we continually receive at Thy bountiful hands; but more especially, with all Thy people assembled this day, we praise Thee that thou didst send into the world Thy Son to save us; and having delivered Him for our offences, didst raise Him up again for our justification, and through His glorious resurrection hast given us the blessed hope of everlasting life.

Here may be introduced any other subject for Thanksgiving.

O Lord, may these our thanksgivings come up with acceptance before Thy throne. Make us worthy at the last day to have part in the resurrection of the just, and the glory of the kingdom of heaven, whither Jesus the Forerunner is for us entered; where now He lives and reigns, and is worshipped and glorified with Thee and the Holy Ghost, God blessed for ever.

For Illumination.

O God, who dost instruct us by Thy Holy Scriptures, we beseech Thee, enlighten our minds and purify our hearts, that we may be able to comprehend, and receive as we ought, the things which are therein revealed to us. Assist Thy ministers that they may proclaim Thy word with purity, clearness, and simplicity. Make their preaching effectual by the virtue of the Holy Spirit, that the good seed may be received into our hearts, as into a soil well prepared, and may bring forth fruits with abundance; that we may not only hear Thy word but keep it, so living in accordance with its divine instructions all the time of our sojourn in this world, that we may come finally to eternal salvation, through Jesus Christ our Lord.

The Lord's Prayer.

Our Father which art in heaven, Hallowed be Thy name. Thy kingdom come. Thy will be done in earth, as it is in heaven. Give us this day our daily bread. And forgive us our trespasses, as we forgive them that trespass against us. And lead us not into temptation; but deliver us from evil: For Thine is the kingdom, and the power, and the glory for ever, and ever.

Amen.

A Sermon is then preached, concluding with an Ascription of Praise; after which a Psalm or Hymn may be sung.
If neither of the Sacraments is to be administered, the Minister then says—

LET US PRAY.

III.

Prayer after Sermon.

ALMIGHTY God, our heavenly Father, grant, we beseech Thee, that the truths which we have now heard may be so rooted in our hearts that they may never be removed, but may produce the fruits of a good and holy life, to the glory of Thy great name, and the advancement of our own salvation.

Here may be introduced any special Prayers, as occasion may require.

Intercessions.

O God, who hast taught us to make supplications, prayers, intercessions, and giving of thanks for all men, we humbly beseech Thee to receive these our prayers, which we offer to Thy divine majesty.

We entreat Thee to bless all princes and governors to whom Thou hast committed the administration of justice, and to grant them the daily increase of Thy good Spirit, that, with true faith acknowledging Thy Son, our Saviour, to be King of kings and Lord of lords, they may serve Thee, exalt Thy rule in their dominions, and so govern their subjects that Thy people everywhere, being kept in peace and quietness, may serve Thee in all godliness and honesty.

Especially we beseech Thee to bless her most sacred Majesty Queen Victoria, and to give her grace so to execute her office that religion may be maintained, manners reformed, and sin punished, according to Thy Word.

Make Thy blessing also to rest upon Albert Edward Prince of Wales, the Princess of Wales, and all the members of the Royal Family.

Grant a spirit of wisdom and of the fear of the Lord to the Queen's counsellors, to the nobles, rulers, and judges of the realm [and to the members of Parliament at this time assembled] [and to the magistrates of this town]; preside in their councils, and so direct all their deliberations that they may promote Thy glory and the public good.

We pray for the prosperity of the Empire and all its dependencies; for favourable weather, plenteous harvests, and peaceful times; for a blessing on our fleets and armies, our trade and commerce, and upon every useful and honest occupation.

Almighty God, King of saints, who hast chosen Zion for Thy habitation and Thy rest for ever, we pray Thee for all whom Thou hast appointed pastors and ministers in Thy Church, [and particularly for him [those] to whom Thou hast given the charge of this flock]. Animate them with Thy Spirit, that they may fulfil their ministry with fidelity and zeal, and labour effectually for the conversion and salvation of souls.

Send forth faithful labourers into Thy harvest; and give Thy grace to those who are preparing to serve Thee in the holy ministry; pour down the healthful influences of Thy Spirit upon all [universities, and] schools of learning, and cause to reign in them that fear of Thee which is the beginning of wisdom.

We beseech Thee on behalf of the Catholic Church, that it may please Thee to protect it everywhere, and to increase and sanctify it more and more; to remove the errors, scandals, and divisions which desolate it, and to reunite all Christians in the bonds of truth, piety, and peace. Particularly we commend to Thee this parish, beseeching Thee to bless all that dwell therein, and to cause all the Christian graces to flourish among them. And forasmuch as Thou wouldst be known as the Saviour of all mankind in the redemption procured by Thy Son Jesus Christ, grant that such as are still strangers to the knowledge of Thee, and plunged in the darkness of ignorance and error, may be illuminated by the light of Thy Gospel, and led into the right way of salvation, which is to know Thee the only true God, and Jesus Christ whom Thou hast sent.

God of all comfort, we commend to Thy mercy all those whom Thou art pleased to visit with any cross or tribulation; the nations whom Thou dost afflict with famine, pestilence, or war; those of our brethren who suffer persecution for the sake of the Gospel; all such as are in danger by sea or land, and all persons oppressed with poverty, sickness, or any other distress of body or sorrow of mind. We pray particularly for the sick and afflicted members of this church, and for those who desire to be remembered in our prayers [and for any such known to ourselves, whom we name in our hearts before Thee]. May it please Thee to show them Thy fatherly kindness, and to deliver them out of all their troubles; above all, grant them the consolations of which they have need, dispose them to patience and resignation, and make their afflictions promote the salvation of their souls.

Finally, O our God and Father, regard with Thy favour this worshipping assembly. Accept our worship, notwithstanding its imperfections; and grant that henceforth, putting all our trust in Thy well-beloved Son, enlightened by His teaching, guided by His example, and sanctified by His Spirit, we may walk in newness of life, and so prepare for that blessed life which Thou hast promised to Thy children in heaven.

Hear us, O merciful Father, in these our supplications, for the sake of Thy dear Son Jesus Christ, our Lord; to whom, with Thee and the Holy Ghost, be all honour and glory, world without end.

Amen.

Then a Psalm or Hymn is sung; and, if convenient, the Alms may be collected. The Minister shall close the service by pronouncing this, or another, of the Benedictions:

The Benediction.

The grace of the Lord Jesus Christ, and the love of God, and the communion of the Holy Ghost, be with you all.

Amen.

Evening Service.

IT is of the Lord's mercies that we are not consumed, and because His compassions fail not.

O magnify the Lord with me, and let us exalt His name together.

I.

Prayer of Invocation.

O LORD our God, we lift up our eyes unto the hills from whence cometh our help. Thou only art the Fountain of life and peace, and in Thy presence is fulness of joy. Father in heaven, from whom cometh down every good and perfect gift, grant us Thy blessing, and incline Thine ear unto us, as we come before Thee in the solemn service of Thy house. Merciful Saviour, who sittest at the right hand of the Father, and makest intercession for us, fulfil now Thy promise: Where two or three are gathered together in my name, there am I in the midst of them. O Holy Ghost, the Comforter, help our infirmities, and enable us to worship in the beauty of holiness; through Christ our Lord.

The Confession.

O God, who hast taught us in Thy holy Word that if we say we have no sin we deceive ourselves, and the truth is not in us; but that if we confess our sins, Thou art faithful and just to forgive us our sins, and to cleanse us from all unrighteousness; receive, we beseech Thee, our humble confessions, through Jesus Christ.

Almighty and most merciful God, our heavenly Father, we cast ourselves down before Thee, under a deep sense of our unworthiness and guilt. We have grievously sinned against Thee in thought, in word, and in deed; we have come short of Thy glory; we have broken Thy commandments, and turned aside every one of us from the way of life, and in us there is no soundness nor health.

Yet now, O most merciful Father, hear us when we call upon Thee with penitent hearts, and for the sake of Thy Son Jesus Christ have mercy upon us. Pardon our sins, and grant us Thy peace. Take away our guilt. Purify us by the inspiration of Thy Holy Spirit from all inward uncleanness, and make us able and willing to serve Thee in newness of life, to the glory of Thy holy name; through Jesus Christ our Lord.

For Pardon and Peace.

We bless Thee, O God, for the comforting assurance of Thy grace, promised in the Gospel, to all who repent and believe: As I live, saith the Lord God, I have no pleasure in the death of the wicked, but that he turn from his way and live. God so loved the world that He gave His only begotten Son, that whosoever believeth on Him should not perish, but have everlasting life.

Grant, therefore, that as many here present as truly repent of their sins, and believe in the Lord Jesus Christ with full purpose of new obedience, may receive now with perfect faith the declaration made by the authority and in the name of Christ, that their sins are forgiven in heaven, according to His promise in the Gospel, through the perfect merit of Jesus Christ our Saviour.

Supplications.

O God, who hast taught us in Thy holy Word to be careful for nothing, but in everything, by prayer and supplication with thanksgiving, to make known our requests unto Thee, give ear unto our prayer, and attend to the voice of our supplication.

O Thou Father of our Lord Jesus Christ, of whom the whole family in heaven and earth is named, we beseech Thee, according to the riches of Thy glory, to strengthen us with might by Thy Spirit in the inner man, that Christ may dwell in our hearts by faith; so that, being rooted and grounded in love, we may be able to comprehend with all saints what is the breadth, and length, and depth, and height, and to know the love of Christ, which passeth knowledge.

God of all power and glory, who hast not appointed us unto wrath, but to obtain salvation by our Lord Jesus Christ, perfect and fulfil in us, we beseech Thee, the work of Thy redeeming mercy. Sanctify us in body, soul, and spirit, and guide us evermore in the way of peace. Help us to overcome the world. Beat down Satan under our feet. Give us courage to confess Christ always, and patience to endure in His service to the end; that, having finished our course with joy, we may rest in hope, and finally attain to the resurrection of the just; through the infinite merits of our Saviour Jesus Christ.

Here may be introduced any other subject for Supplication.

Give ear, O Lord, unto our prayer. Keep us now and always in Thy faith and fear; and so cleanse our conscience, we beseech Thee, by the daily visitation of Thy grace, that when Thy Son our Lord shall come, He may find us fit for His appearing, and ready to meet Him, without spot, in the company of all His saints; who liveth and reigneth with Thee and the Holy Ghost, ever one God, world without end.

Amen.

II.

The Thanksgiving.

WE will bless the Lord at all times: His praise shall continually be in our mouth.

O God, Giver of all good, and Fountain of all mercies, in whom are the springs of our life; all glory, thanks, and praise be unto Thee for thine ever-flowing goodness; for Thy faithfulness which is from one generation to another; for Thy mercies which are new every morning, fresh every moment, and more than we can number; for seed-time and harvest, and summer and winter, and nights and days throughout the year; for food, and raiment, and shelter; for health and reason; for childhood and age, and youth and manhood; for Thy fatherly hand ever upon us in sickness and in health, in joy and in sorrow, in life and in death; for friends, and kindred, and kind benefactors; for home and country; for Thy Church and for Thy Gospel.

Here may be introduced any other subject for Thanksgiving.

Yea, Lord, for that there is nothing for which we may not bless and thank Thee, therefore do we call upon Thy name, and pay our vows now in the presence of all Thy people, humbly beseeching Thee to accept our service, even as we offer it in the name and through the infinite merits of Thy Son Jesus Christ, our Lord.

For Illumination.

Cause Thy Church to arise and shine, O Lord, and let her ministers be clothed with righteousness and salvation; that Thy word which is in their hands may not return unto Thee void, but have free course and be glorified in the world; prospering in the thing whereunto Thou hast sent it, and prevailing mightily to turn men from darkness to light, and from the power of Satan unto God, that they may receive the forgiveness of sins, and inheritance among them which are sanctified, by faith that is in Christ; to whom, with Thee and the Holy Ghost, be honour and glory, world without end.

The Lord's Prayer.

Our Father which art in heaven, Hallowed be Thy name. Thy kingdom come. Thy will be done in earth, as it is in heaven. Give us this day our daily bread. And forgive us our trespasses, as we forgive them that trespass against us. And lead us not into temptation; but deliver us from evil: For Thine is the kingdom, and the power, and the glory for ever and ever.
 𝔄men.

III.

Prayer after Sermon.

O GOD, who didst teach the hearts of Thy faithful people, by sending to them the light of Thy Holy Spirit, grant us, by the same Spirit, to have a right understanding of Thy saving truth. Visit, we pray Thee, this congregation with Thy love and favour; enlighten our minds more and more with the light of the everlasting Gospel; graft in our hearts a love of the truth; increase in us true religion; nourish us with all goodness; and of Thy great mercy keep us in the same; through Jesus Christ our Lord.

Here may be introduced any special Prayers, as occasion may require.

Intercessions.

O God, who hast taught us, by Thy holy apostle, that we should make supplications, prayers, intercessions, and giving of thanks for all people, mercifully hear the petitions which we offer to Thee on behalf of others.

Almighty God, King of kings, and Lord of lords, from whom proceedeth all power and dominion in heaven and on earth, most heartily we beseech Thee to look with favour upon her most sacred Majesty Queen Victoria, Albert Edward Prince of Wales, the Princess of Wales, and all the members of the Royal Family,

Imbue all in authority with the spirit of wisdom, goodness, and truth, and so rule their hearts and bless their endeavours, that law and order, justice and peace, may everywhere prevail.

Preserve us from public calamities; from pestilence and famine; from war, privy conspiracy, and rebellion; but especially from national sins and corruption. Make us strong and great in the fear of God, and in the love of righteousness; so, that, being blessed of Thee, we may become a blessing to all nations, to the praise of the glory of Thy grace; through Jesus Christ.

O Thou God and Father of our Lord Jesus Christ, of whom the whole family in heaven and earth is named, cause Thy blessing, we beseech Thee, to rest upon the Church, which He has purchased with His most precious blood. Illuminate her ministers with true knowledge, and understanding of Thy Word. Send down the healthful dew of Thy grace upon all her congregations. Deliver her from false doctrine, heresy, and schism; and clothe her with the beauty of holiness and peace. Reveal Thy glory among all nations; destroy all wicked devices formed against Thy Holy Word; and bring in speedily the full victory of Thine everlasting kingdom; through Jesus Christ our Lord.

O God, the Creator and Preserver of all mankind, we implore Thy mercy in behalf of all classes and conditions of men, that it may please Thee to visit them with Thy most compassionate help, according to their manifold necessities and wants. Especially we beseech Thee to show pity upon all widows and orphans, upon all prisoners and captives, upon all sick and dying persons, upon those who are desolate or sore afflicted in any way, and upon all such as are persecuted for righteousness' sake. Enable them to look unto Thee, O most merciful Father, and to call upon Thy name, that they may find Thee a present Saviour in their affliction and distress; and let it please Thee to deliver them, and raise them up in due time, giving them patience under all their sufferings, the rich comfort of Thy grace here below, and eternal rest with Thee in heaven; through our Lord Jesus Christ.

Almighty God, our heavenly Father, we render Thee hearty thanks that Thou hast permitted us once more to enter the courts of Thy sanctuary, to hear Thy Word, to sing Thy praise, to enjoy the communion of saints, and to be built up in our most holy faith, on the foundation of the apostles and prophets. Continue to us the use of the precious means of grace, and grant that we all who are now assembled in Thy sanctuary on earth, may be numbered with the saints in glory everlasting, and may render praise unto Thee the Father, the Son, and the Holy Ghost, God blessed for evermore.

Amen.

The Benediction.

The grace of the Lord Jesus Christ, and the love of God, and the communion of the Holy Ghost, be with you all.

Amen.

Second Sunday of the Month.

Morning Service.

THE Lord is in His holy temple: let all the earth keep silence before Him.

O come, let us worship and bow down; let us kneel before the Lord our Maker. For He is our God; and we are the people of His pasture, and the sheep of His hand.

I.

Prayer of Invocation.

O THOU who hast made the Church Thy dwelling-place, and chosen it as Thy rest for ever, and hast taught us in Thy Word not to forsake the assembling of ourselves together; regard in special mercy, we beseech Thee, us Thy servants, who meet this day in Thy holy courts. Manifest Thyself unto us as Thou dost not unto the world, and so bless unto us all

Thine ordinances, that our worship may prepare us both to serve Thee now, and to glorify Thee hereafter, in Thine eternal kingdom; through Jesus Christ our Lord.

The Confession.

If we say we have no sin, we deceive ourselves, and the truth is not in us. If we confess our sins, Thou art faithful and just to forgive us our sins, and to cleanse us from all unrighteousness.

We confess, O God, that we have sinned against Thee, and are unworthy of Thy mercy. We have not loved Thee, our Father; we have grieved the Holy Ghost, the earnest of our inheritance; we have not desired the coming of Thy Son Jesus Christ our Lord. We have not been pure and holy; we have not been faithful and true; we have been entangled in the world, and overcome of evil. We have lived in confusion and strife; we have done wrong unto our brother, and have not repented of the wrong; we have broken the unity of Thy holy Church, and caused men to forget and blaspheme Thy name. Our faith hath failed us; our love hath grown cold; our hope hath not been as an anchor of the soul sure and steadfast, entering within the veil. We remember these things before Thee; we cast ourselves upon Thy compassion; we cry unto Thee, Be merciful unto us, sinners. Hear us for the sake of Jesus Christ, who died for us upon the cross, and who rose again for our justification; that, obtaining of Thee forgiveness of all our sins, and being filled with Thy Holy Spirit, we may be enabled evermore to glorify Thee in our body and our spirit, which are Thine.

For Pardon and Peace.

Almighty and everlasting God, who hatest nothing that Thou hast made, and dost forgive the sins of all them that are penitent; create and make in us new and contrite hearts, that we, who have lamented our sins, and acknowledged our wretchedness, may obtain of Thee, the God of all mercy, perfect remission and forgiveness; through Jesus Christ our Lord.

Supplications.

Give ear, O Lord, unto our prayer, and attend to the voice of our supplication.

Grant us to pass all the days of our life in peace and holiness, without sin and stumbling.

Enable us to perform our allotted tasks with diligence, to guide our affairs with discretion, and in all our ways to acknowledge Thee.

Feed us with food convenient for us; bestow upon us health of body and soundness of mind; and further our lawful undertakings with Thy blessing.

Restrain us from all intemperance and excess, from all vanity in speech and behaviour; and make us sober and watchful to prayer.

O God, the Fountain of all truth and grace, who hast called us out of darkness into marvellous light by the glorious Gospel of Thy Son, grant unto us power, we beseech Thee, to walk worthy of our vocation, with all lowliness and meekness, endeavouring to keep the unity of the spirit in the bond of peace; that we may have our fruit unto holiness, and the end everlasting life; through Jesus Christ our Lord.

O God, who didst suffer Thine own Son to be tempted of the wicked one, that He might be able to succour them that are tempted, we beseech Thee to deliver us from those snares and temptations by which we are continually beset: save us from the spirit of guile and deceit; from the spirit of malice and uncharitableness; from the spirit of falsehood and uncleanness; and so strengthen us mightily by Thy good Spirit, that in all things we may be more than conquerors through Him that loved us, and washed us from our sins in His own blood.

Here may be introduced any other subject for Supplication.

O Thou who bestowest liberally and upbraidest not, be pleased now, for Thy Son's sake, to give unto us those things which we have asked in His name, and to forgive our unworthiness in asking. Evermore pardon all our sins; deliver us from all evil; preserve us in the faith and fear of Thy holy name unto our life's end; keep us watchful for the coming of Thy Son; and bring us at last into Thy heavenly kingdom; through Jesus Christ our Lord.

𝔄men.

II.

The Thanksgiving.

O LORD, open Thou our lips; and our mouth shall show forth Thy praise.

It is a good thing to give thanks unto Thee, O God; to show forth Thy loving-kindness in the morning, and Thy faithfulness every night.

We thank Thee for all the bounties of Thy providence; for health and strength, for food and raiment; for health and succour in times of need, for pity and consolation in times of sorrow; and for all the kindness Thou hast shown us from the beginning of our days until now. But above all, we thank Thee for Thine infinite love to us, miserable sinners; that Thou hast given Thy Son to be the propitiation for our sins; that Thou hast sent down Thy Holy Spirit to sanctify our corrupt natures; that Thou hast called us out of darkness into the marvellous light of Thy Gospel; that Thou hast favoured us with the means of grace, and hast comforted us with the hope of glory.

Here may be introduced any other subject for Thanksgiving.

Help us, we beseech Thee, to acknowledge Thy goodness, in all time to come, by trusting entirely in Thee, by contentment with the portion Thou hast given us, by charity to the poor and needy, and by a cheerful obedience to Thy holy commandments.

For Illumination.

O Lord, who alone canst give the hearing ear and the understanding heart; open our minds, we beseech Thee, to understand Thy Word, which Thou hast in Thy mercy bestowed upon us. Save us from using Thy Word deceitfully; from wresting it to serve our own purpose; from being in bondage to the letter while we neglect the spirit. But grant that we may search the Scriptures diligently, and find in them their testimony to Christ; and beholding His glory reflected in them, may be changed into it ever more and more, till we are made like Him in His heavenly kingdom; through the same Jesus Christ our Lord.

The Lord's Prayer.

Our Father which art in heaven, Hallowed be Thy name. Thy kingdom come. Thy will be done in earth, as it is in heaven. Give us this day our daily bread. And forgive us our trespasses, as we forgive them that trespass against us. And lead us not into temptation; but deliver us from evil: For Thine is the kingdom, and the power, and the glory for ever, and ever.
𝔄men.

III.

Prayer after Sermon.

O GOD, who hast sounded in our ears Thy divine and saving oracles; enlighten our souls to the full understanding of what has been spoken, that we may not only be hearers of spiritual words, but doers also of good works;

following after faith unfeigned, blameless life, and conversation without reproach; through Jesus Christ our Lord.

Here may be introduced any special Prayers, as occasion may require.

Intercessions.

O God, who hast taught us to make supplications, prayers, intercessions, and giving of thanks for all men, we humbly beseech Thee to receive these our prayers, which we offer to Thy divine majesty.

We pray for Thy servant her most sacred Majesty Queen Victoria, that it may please Thee to grant her Thy Holy Spirit, that she may, with a pure faith, acknowledge Thee, and give herself wholly to please Thee, and to advance Thy kingdom in her dominions. We pray Thee to bless Albert Edward Prince of Wales, the Princess of Wales, and all the members of the Royal Family.

We pray [for the High Court of Parliament now assembled, and] for all rulers, judges, and magistrates [and especially for those of this town], that Thou wouldst give the spirit of wisdom to those to whom Thou hast given the authority of government; and that we, under those set over us, may lead quiet and peaceable lives, in all godliness and honesty.

We pray for Thy Holy Catholic Church upon earth, that, guided with Thy perpetual governance, she may walk warily in times of quiet, and boldly in times of trouble; that those who love her may abide in her peace, and those who depart from her may be restored to her fellowship; and that when all sorrows are taken away, we may have part in the joys of an eternal resurrection.

We pray for those who minister in holy things [and particularly for him [those] to whom Thou hast given the charge of this flock]; let Thy power come to the aid of Thy servants, and clothe them with glory and beauty; and so perfect Thy gifts in them, that they may faithfully discharge their ministry according to Thy pleasure, and at the last may enter into Thy heavenly rest.

We pray Thee to deliver the heathen from idolatry, and gather them into Thy fold; that, by acknowledging the Light which is Christ, they may be rescued from their own darkness.

We pray for those who wander in doubt and uncertainty amid the darkness of this evil world, and for all who are hardened through the deceitfulness of sin: vouchsafe them grace to come to themselves; the will and the power to return unto Thee; and the loving welcome of Thy forgiveness.

We pray for all in sickness and distress, [and

for any such known to ourselves whom we name in our hearts before Thee ;] that Thou wouldst give strength to the weary, aid to the sufferers, comfort to the sad, and help to all in tribulation.

We pray Thee for the dying, that the souls of Thy servants may be released in peace, and that, dying to the world, they may live for evermore to Thee.

Be present, O Lord, to our prayers, and protect us by day and by night; keep us watchful for the appearing of Thy beloved Son; and grant that in all successive changes of times, we may ever be strengthened by Thine unchangeableness, through Jesus Christ our Lord; to whom with Thee, and the Holy Ghost, be the glory, as it was in the beginning, is now, and ever shall be, world without end.

Amen.

The Benediction.

The grace of the Lord Jesus Christ, and the love of God, and the communion of the Holy Ghost, be with you all.

Amen.

Evening Service.

THE hour cometh, and now is, when the true worshippers shall worship the Father in spirit and in truth; for the Father seeketh such to worship Him. God is a spirit; and they that worship Him must worship Him in spirit and in truth.

O worship the Lord in the beauty of holiness: fear before Him all the earth.

I.

Prayer of Invocation.

O GOD, Light of the hearts that see Thee, and Life of the souls that love Thee, and Strength of the thoughts that seek Thee; from whom to be turned away is to fall, to whom to be turned is to rise, and in whom to abide is to stand fast for ever: grant us now Thy grace and blessing, as we are here assembled to offer up our common supplications; and though we are unworthy to approach Thee, or to ask anything of Thee at all, vouchsafe to hear and to answer us, for the sake of our great High Priest and Advocate, Jesus Christ our Lord.

The Confession.

We have sinned against Thee, and have done wickedly. Our thoughts have been evil and vain continually. Our hearts have been deceitful above all things, and desperately wicked. Our members have been the instruments of unrighteousness to sin. We have not loved Thee with a pure heart fervently, neither have we loved our neighbour as ourselves. We have not done justly, or loved mercy, or walked humbly with Thee, our God; but we have been greedy of sin and impatient of reproof, and Thee we have not glorified. We confess our sins before Thee: sins that are secret and sins that are open; sins that are forgotten and sins that are remembered; infinite in their degrees, intolerable in their load, we confess them all before Thee.

Enter not into judgment with Thy servants, O Lord: for in Thy sight shall no flesh living be justified.

Have mercy upon us, O Lord, according to Thy loving-kindness; according to the multitude of Thy tender mercies, blot out our iniquity.

Return, O Lord, how long? and let it repent Thee concerning Thy servants.

Have pity on us, have pity on us, according to Thy great mercy in Christ Jesus our Lord.

For Pardon and Peace.

O Thou gracious Father of mercy, Father of our Lord Jesus Christ, have mercy upon Thy servants who bow before Thee; pardon and forgive us all our sins; give us the grace of true repentance, and a strict obedience to Thy holy Word; strengthen us in the inner man for all the parts and duties of holy living; preserve us for ever in the unity of Thy holy Church, in the integrity of the Christian faith, in the love of Thee and of our neighbours, in the hope of eternal life, and in Thy peace which passeth all understanding.

Supplications.

Hear us, O Lord, when we cry unto Thee, for unto Thee do we lift up our souls.

We renounce the works of darkness; cause us to walk in the light of Thy countenance. We renounce the vanities of this world; help us to seek after the enduring substance laid up with Thee in heaven. We renounce the sinful lusts of the flesh; enable us to walk in the Spirit.

Teach us to endure hardness as good soldiers of Jesus Christ, that we may not fear the reproach of men, nor be ashamed of Christ or of His cross; and that we may not count life itself dear unto us, so we may finish our course with joy.

Quicken us to work the works of Him that hath sent us, while it is day, because the night cometh wherein no man can work; and what we do, enable us to do it heartily, as unto the Lord, and not unto men.

Grant us, in all our duties, Thy help; in all our difficulties, Thy counsel; in all our dangers, Thy protection; and in all our sorrows, Thy peace.

Almighty God, our most holy and eternal Father, who art of pure eyes, and canst behold no iniquity, let Thy gracious and holy Spirit descend upon Thy servants; that no impure thoughts may pollute that soul which Thou hast sanctified, no impure words pollute that tongue which Thou hast ordained an organ of Thy praise, no impure action rend the veil of that temple which Thou hast chosen for an habitation; but grant that, our senses being sealed up from all vain objects, our hearts entirely possessed with religion, fortified with prudence, watchfulness, and self-denial, we may so live in this present world as not to fail of the glories of the world to come.

Here may be introduced any other subject for Supplication.

O Lord most mighty and most merciful, we commend ourselves unto Thee and to the Word of Thy grace, which is able to build us up and to give us an inheritance among all them that are sanctified. We beseech Thee to keep our souls from death, our eyes from tears, and our feet from falling, that we may walk before Thee in the light of the living, and at the second and glorious appearing of Thy Son our Lord, may be presented faultless before the presence of Thy glory with exceeding joy; through the same Jesus Christ our Saviour.

Almighty Father, who art the hearer of prayer, unto whom all flesh shall come, be pleased to pardon what has been amiss in these our supplications. Forgive our wandering and unholy thoughts; accept of us, and receive our offering, and let Thy blessing be upon us for evermore; through Jesus Christ our Lord.

Amen.

II.

The Thanksgiving.

WE praise and bless Thy holy name, Father of mercies and God of all grace, as for all Thy temporal mercies, so especially that

Thou hast had compassion upon us, miserable sinners: that Thou didst send Thy Son to seek and save us: that He took on Him the form of a servant, and the likeness of sinful flesh, and fulfilled Thy law, and was obedient to all Thy will, even unto death: that He made propitiation for our sins: and when he had overcome the sharpness of death, He opened the kingdom of heaven to all believers: that He sitteth at Thy right hand in glory everlasting: that He will come again in majesty to judge the quick and the dead: and will reign till all enemies are put under His feet: that He is our Advocate with Thee, the Captain of our salvation, the Author and Finisher of the faith: that He is our light, and life, and hope: that He is not untouched with the feeling of our infirmities, having been in all points tempted as we are: that He ever liveth to make intercession, and saveth to the uttermost them that come unto Thee by Him: that Thou hast sent unto us Thy Holy Spirit, and the Gospel of Thy grace: and hast permitted us in peace and safety to enjoy another of the days of the Son of Man upon the earth, to unite with Thy Church militant in calling upon Thy name, and learning the way of eternal life; through our Lord and Saviour Jesus Christ.

Here may be introduced any other subject for Thanksgiving.

For Illumination.

Let Thy Gospel, O Lord, come unto us not in word only but in power, and in much assurance, and in the Holy Ghost, that we may be guided into all truth, and strengthened unto all obedience and enduring of Thy will with joyfulness; that, abounding in the work of faith, and the labour of love, and the patience of hope, we may finally be made meet to be partakers of the inheritance of the saints in light; through Jesus Christ our Lord.

The Lord's Prayer.

Our Father which art in heaven, Hallowed be Thy name. Thy kingdom come. Thy will be done in earth, as it is in heaven. Give us this day our daily bread. And forgive us our trespasses, as we forgive them that trespass against us. And lead us not into temptation; but deliver us from evil: For Thine is the kingdom, and the power, and the glory for ever and ever.

Amen.

III.

Prayer after Sermon.

SUFFER not, O God, the good seed, which the Son of Man hath sown, to be caught away by the wicked one out of our hearts, or to be scorched by tribulation or persecution, or to be choked with cares and pleasures of this life; but being received into good and honest hearts, may it bring forth in us abundantly the fruits of faith and obedience; through our Lord and Saviour Jesus Christ.

Here may be introduced any special Prayers, as occasion may require.

Intercessions.

Remember, O Lord, all those whom Thou hast made to reign upon the earth, especially Thy servant her most sacred Majesty Queen Victoria. Bless Albert Edward Prince of Wales, the Princess of Wales, and all the Royal Family. With the helmet of salvation, with the crown of Thy good pleasure, endue them, O Lord; exalt their right hand; establish their kingdom. Give them a deep peace that none can take away; and rule in their hearts for the good of Thy Church, and of all Thy people.

O God, from whom cometh down every good and perfect gift, hear us when we beseech Thee to remember Thy Holy Catholic and Apostolic Church. Give peace to her whom Thou hast purchased with the precious blood of Thy Christ, and establish Thy holy house to the end of the world.

Remember, O Lord, all who bear rule in Thy Church, who rightly divide Thy word of truth; and let none be confounded who minister at Thy holy altar.

Remember, O Lord, those who bring forth fruit, and do good works in Thy Church, and who remember the poor. Recompense them with rich and heavenly gifts. Render to them, instead of earthly things, the heavenly; instead of the temporal, the eternal; instead of corruptible, the incorruptible.

Remember, O Lord, the whole body of the people; all those present before Thee, and those who are absent for a reasonable cause; and have compassion upon them, and upon us, according to the multitude of Thy mercies. Fill their stores with every good thing; keep Thou their families in peace and concord; bring up their little ones; teach the young; strengthen the old; comfort the disheartened; gather those who are scattered, and bring back those who have gone astray; go Thou with the travellers by sea and land; care Thou for the widows;

protect the orphans; deliver the captives; heal the sick.

Remember, O Lord, those who are in any tribulation, necessity, or danger; all those who are in need of Thy great compassions; those who love us or hate us; those who have given us charge, unworthy as we are, to pray for them; and those whom we through ignorance or forgetfulness remember not: do Thou, O Lord, who knowest the state and occupation of every one, remember them. Be Thou all to all, who knowest each heart and its request, each house and its need. Keep the righteous in righteousness; make the wicked good through Thy goodness.

Visit us in Thy kindness; manifest Thyself unto us in Thy love. Grant us temperate and favourable seasons; deliver us from fire and pestilence; from famine and sword. Appease the dissensions of the Churches; bring to nought the risings of heresies; repress the tumults of the nations.

Receive us all into Thine eternal kingdom, showing us to be children of the light and of the day; and grant us now and evermore Thy peace and Thy love, O Lord our God, for Thou alone hast given, and givest us, all things.

Thine is the day, O Lord, and Thine is the night; grant that the Sun of Righteousness may remain in our hearts, to drive away the darkness of wicked thoughts: through Jesus Christ our Lord; to whom with Thee, the Father, and the Holy Ghost, be the glory, as it was in the beginning, is now, and ever shall be, world without end.

Amen.

The Benediction.

The grace of the Lord Jesus Christ, and the love of God, and the communion of the Holy Ghost, be with you all.

Amen.

Third Sunday of the Month.

Morning Service.

THE Lord is high above all nations, and His glory above the heavens. Who is like unto the Lord our God, who dwelleth on high, who humbleth Himself to behold the things that are in heaven, and in the earth?

We have not an High Priest that cannot be touched with the feeling of our infirmities; but was in all points tempted like as we are, yet without sin. Let us therefore come boldly unto the throne of grace, that we may obtain mercy, and find grace to help in time of need.

I.

Prayer of Invocation.

O LORD God, merciful and holy, who didst command light to shine out of darkness, who hast given us rest in sleep, and hast raised us up to glorify Thee and to declare Thy goodness; we beseech Thee of Thy great mercy to accept us who now worship before Thee, and according to our power do give Thee thanks, and to grant unto us our requests for all things pertaining to our everlasting salvation; through Jesus Christ our Lord.

The Confession.

If we say we have no sin, we deceive ourselves, and the truth is not in us. If we confess our sins, Thou art faithful and just to forgive us our sins, and to cleanse us from all unrighteousness.

We, poor sinners, confess before Thee, our Lord, God, and Creator, that from our youth until this present time, we have greatly sinned in thought, in word, and in deed, neglecting the good and doing the evil, as Thou the searcher of hearts well knowest, and as we cannot enough deplore. We do repent, and are heartily sorry. We beseech Thy mercy. O Lord, merciful God, forgive our transgressions for the sake of the life and death of our Lord Jesus Christ, our only Mediator with Thee. As we from the heart forgive them that have sinned against us, do Thou show the like mercy unto us, and to all penitent sinners, and of Thy pity lead and guide us all from the misery of sin unto eternal life; through Jesus Christ our Lord.

For Pardon and Peace.

Almighty God, the Father of our Lord Jesus Christ, who hast given us grace at this time to confess our sins unto Thee, grant unto us full remission and forgiveness, and absolve us from all our sins, iniquities, and transgressions; give unto us peace through Thy Word of pardon proclaimed unto us in His name; and vouchsafe unto us the inspiration of Thy Holy Spirit, that at this time we may offer unto Thee true and acceptable worship; that for the time to come we may serve and please Thee in righteousness and true holiness; and that at the appearing of our Lord Jesus Christ we may be found of Him in peace unto salvation.

Supplications.

Give ear, O Lord, unto our prayer, and attend to the voice of our supplication.

Pour out upon us the gifts of the Holy Ghost. Grant unto us an unreprovable faith, a just and humble hope, and a never-failing charity. Grant unto us the grace of true humility, a meek and quiet spirit, pure and holy thoughts, clear understanding in the way of godliness, and a holy and edifying conversation.

Grant unto us to deny ourselves; to bear the burden of others; to be slow to anger; to fight manfully the battles of the Lord against the flesh, the world, and the devil; to redeem the time; and to walk always as in Thy presence.

Grant unto us spiritual wisdom, that we may discern what is pleasing to Thee, and follow what belongs to our peace; and let the knowledge and love of Thee and of Jesus Christ our Lord be our guide and our portion all our days. Sanctify us in spirit, soul, and body, and preserve us blameless unto the coming of our Lord and King.

Here may be introduced any other subject for Supplication.

Incline, O Lord, we beseech Thee, Thine ear to our prayers, and visit the darkness of our mind with the dayspring from on high; that at the second coming of Thy Son to judge the world, we may hasten with joy to meet Him, who liveth and reigneth with Thee and the Holy Ghost, ever one God, world without end.

Amen.

II.

The Thanksgiving.

O LORD, open Thou our lips; and our mouth shall show forth Thy praise.

We give thanks unto Thee, O God of our salvation, that Thou hast crowned our lives with Thy mercies; we look unto Thee as the Saviour and benefactor of our souls. Thou didst create heaven and earth, and all things that are therein. Thou gavest unto us life and being. By Thy providence are the fruits of the earth preserved to us; and by Thy blessing we, and all things living, are nourished and sustained. Thou openest Thine hand and fillest us with plenty. Thou hast preserved us all our days, and now again Thou bringest us into Thy presence, in the multitude of Thy mercies, and replenished with Thy goodness.

But above all, Thou hast loved us and all mankind when we were lost; and hast given Thine only begotten Son to seek and save us. We bless Thee for His love and condescension, for His immaculate holiness, for His perfect example, for His bitter passion and His death upon the cross, for His triumph over death and hell, for His glorious resurrection and ascension, for His intercession and rule at Thy right hand.

We thank Thee for the giving of the Holy Ghost; for the Church which Thou hast planted among us; for its ministries and means of grace; for the promises and precepts of Thy holy Word; and for all the helps and comforts of true religion.

Here may be introduced any other subject for Thanksgiving.

Help us with our whole soul evermore to praise Thee, and to live worthy of these Thy benefits.

For Illumination.

O Lord and lover of men, cause the pure light of Thy divine knowledge to shine forth in our hearts, and open the eyes of our understandings, that we may comprehend the precepts of Thy Gospel. Plant in us also the fear of Thy blessed commandments; that we, trampling upon all fleshly lusts, may seek a heavenly citizenship, both saying and doing always such things as shall please Thee.

The Lord's Prayer.

Our Father which art in heaven, Hallowed be Thy name. Thy kingdom come. Thy will be done in earth, as it is in heaven. Give us this day our daily bread. And forgive us our trespasses, as we forgive them that trespass against us. And lead us not into temptation; but deliver us from evil: For Thine is the kingdom, and the power, and the glory for ever and ever.

Amen.

III.

Prayer after Sermon.

O ALMIGHTY God, who hast begotten us through Thy Word, renewed us by Thy Spirit, nourished us by Thy sacraments, and by the ministry of Thy Church, be pleased still to build us up to life eternal. Give us understanding in Thy law, that we may know Thy will, and grace and strength faithfully to fulfil the same. Grant that our understandings may know Thee, our hearts may love Thee, and all our faculties and powers give Thee due obedience and service; so that, escaping from the darkness of this world, we may at length come to the land of everlasting rest, in Thy light to behold light and glory; through Jesus Christ our Lord.

Here may be introduced any special Prayers, as occasion may require.

Intercessions.

O God, who hast taught us to make supplications, prayers, intercessions, and giving of thanks for all men, we beseech Thee to receive these our prayers which we offer humbly to Thy divine majesty.

In mercy remember her most sacred Majesty the Queen; preserve her person in health and honour, her crown in wealth and dignity, her kingdom in peace and plenty, the Churches under her protection in piety and knowledge, and a strict and holy religion: keep her perpetually in Thy fear and favour, and crown her with glory and immortality.

Make Thy blessing also to rest upon Albert Edward Prince of Wales, the Princess of Wales, and all the members of the Royal Family.

Grant a spirit of wisdom and of the fear of the Lord to the Queen's counsellors, to the nobles, rulers, and judges of the realm [and to the members of Parliament at this time assembled] [and to the magistrates of this town]; preside in their councils, and so direct all their doings and deliberations, that they may promote Thy glory and the public good.

O almighty and most merciful Father, who hast loved Thine elect with an everlasting love, and purchased them unto Thyself with the blood of Thy dear Son; favourably regard, we beseech Thee, Thy Church and congregation [and particularly him [those] to whom Thou hast given the charge of this flock], and confirm them evermore with all spiritual gifts. And grant that the whole company of the faithful may abide steadfast in the faith, abounding in hope, of one heart and of one mind, and filled with joy and with the Holy Ghost.

In mercy remember the poor and needy, the widows and the fatherless, the strangers and the friendless, the sick and the dying [and any such known to ourselves whom we name in our hearts before Thee]; relieve their needs, comfort their sorrows, sanctify their sufferings, strengthen their weakness, and in due time bring them from their bondage into the glorious liberty of the sons of God.

Visit, we beseech Thee, O Lord, our habitations with Thy mercy, and us Thy servants with salvation. Let Thy holy angels watch over us, and let Thy Spirit illuminate our souls. Let no evil overtake us, and let Thy blessing abide on us for ever; through Jesus Christ our Lord.

O Lord our God, who hast shown great mercy to us Thy sinful and unworthy servants, upon whom Thy holy name is called, put us not to shame for our hope in Thee; but grant us, Lord, all these our petitions, and count us worthy to love and fear Thee with all our hearts, and to do in all things Thy most holy will. For Thou, O God, art good, and lovest all mankind. And to Thee we ascribe all glory, to the Father, and to the Son, and to the Holy Ghost, now and for evermore.

Amen.

The Benediction.

The grace of the Lord Jesus Christ, and the love of God, and the communion of the Holy Ghost, be with you all.

Amen.

Evening Service.

OUR help cometh from the Lord, which made heaven and earth. He will not suffer our feet to be moved: He that keepeth us will not slumber. Behold, He that keepeth Israel shall neither slumber nor sleep.

Trust in Him at all times, ye people; pour out your heart before Him; God is a refuge for us.

I.

Prayer of Invocation.

O LORD our God, of boundless might and incomprehensible glory, measureless compassion and infinite love to man; look down on us and on this holy place, and show unto us and to them that pray with us the riches of Thy mercies and compassions; and so make us worthy, with a pure heart and a broken spirit, with hallowed lips and with a countenance that needeth not to be ashamed, to call upon Thee; through Jesus Christ our Lord.

The Confession.

He that covereth his sins shall not prosper; but he that confesseth and forsaketh his sins shall have mercy.

Almighty and most merciful Father, we acknowledge and bewail our manifold sins and wickedness which we from time to time, and especially in the course of the past day, most grievously have committed, by thought, word, and deed, against Thy divine majesty, provoking most justly Thy wrath and indignation against us. We have broken the vows made unto Thee in our baptism, wherein we were made members of the body of Thy Son Jesus Christ; we have separated ourselves from one another, disregarding the unity of Thy holy Church; we have not held fast the hope of the coming and kingdom of our Lord, and we have not purified ourselves as He is pure; we have not worthily praised Thee for Thy goodness, nor rendered unto Thee the glory due unto Thy holy name.

For Pardon and Peace.

Almighty God, and most merciful Father, who delightest not in the death of a sinner, but rather that he be converted from his sin and live; give unto Thy servants a deep contrition for their sins, a perfect hatred, and a full remission of them; visit us with the joys of Thy salvation, and the sweet sense that Thine anger is turned away from us; grant unto us grace to fear and love Thee, power and will to serve Thee, and time and space to finish the work which Thou hast given us to do; that we, being sprinkled with the blood of the Lamb of God, may be justified by Thy grace, sanctified by Thy Spirit, and saved by Thine infinite and eternal goodness; through Jesus Christ our Lord.

Supplications.

Almighty God, the Fountain of all holiness, who by Thy Word and Spirit dost conduct all Thy servants in the way of peace and righteousness, inviting them by Thy promises, winning them by Thy long-suffering, and endearing them by Thy loving-kindness; grant unto us so truly to repent us of our sins, so carefully to reform our errors, so diligently to watch over all our actions, so industriously to perform all our duty, that we may never willingly transgress Thy holy laws: but that it may be the work of our lives to obey Thee, the joy of our souls to please Thee, the satisfaction of all our hopes and the perfection of all our desires to live with

Thee, in the holiness of Thy kingdom of grace and glory; through Jesus Christ our Lord.

Here may be introduced any other subject for Supplication.

Visit and cleanse our consciences, we beseech Thee, O Lord, that when Thy Son Jesus Christ shall come He may find us fit and ready for His appearing, not sleeping in our sins, but awake and rejoicing in His praises.

Hasten, O God, the time when Thou shalt send from Thy right hand Him whom Thou wilt send; at whose glorious appearing Thy saints departed shall be raised, and they which are alive and remain shall be caught up to meet Him, and so shall ever be with the Lord.

O Lord God, who givest to men the blessed hope of eternal life by our Lord Jesus Christ, and hast promised Thy Holy Spirit to them that ask Him; be present with us, and with all Thy ministers and people, in the dispensation of Thy holy Word; and grant that our worship, being offered in the name and in the Spirit of Thy Son, may be acceptable unto Thee and profitable unto ourselves; through our only Mediator and Advocate, Jesus Christ our Lord.

Amen.

II.

The Thanksgiving.

O THOU whom cherubim and seraphim continually do praise, the heavens and all the powers therein, we offer unto Thee our thanksgiving for all Thy goodness.

We bless Thee that Thou hast made us after Thine own image; that Thou hast spared us hitherto, and brought us to the worship of Thy holy name; that Thou hast preserved us safe amidst the changes of this mortal life, and hast supplied our wants out of Thy fulness. But especially do we bless Thee for sending Thy Son Jesus Christ into the world to lighten our darkness, and lead us unto heavenly truth. We bless Thee for His holy incarnation, for His life on earth, for His precious sufferings and death upon the cross, for His resurrection from the dead, for His glorious ascension to Thy right hand, whence He shall come again to judge the quick and the dead. We bless Thee for the giving of the Holy Ghost, for all the sacraments and ordinances of Thy Church, for the communion of saints, for the forgiveness of sins, for the resurrection of the body, and for the life everlasting.

Here may be introduced any other subject for Thanksgiving.

Thee, mighty God, heavenly King, we magnify and praise. With angels and archangels, and with all the company of heaven, we laud and magnify Thy glorious name: evermore praising Thee, and saying, Holy, holy, holy, Lord God of hosts; heaven and earth are full of Thy glory: glory be to Thee, O Lord most high.

For Illumination.

O God, who hast promised that in the last days the mountain of the Lord's house shall be exalted above the hills, and all nations shall flow unto it; send forth Thy light and Thy truth now unto Thy servants; leading them in the paths of Thine ordinances, and in the ways of Thy commandments; that we and Thy whole Church, perfect in every member, complete in holiness and instructed in righteousness, may be presented before Thee without spot or blemish, in the day of the appearing and kingdom of the Lord Jesus.

The Lord's Prayer.

Our Father which art in heaven, Hallowed be Thy name. Thy kingdom come. Thy will be done in earth, as it is in heaven. Give us this day our daily bread. And forgive us our trespasses, as we forgive them that trespass against us. And lead us not into temptation; but deliver us from evil: For Thine is the kingdom, and the power, and the glory for ever and ever.

Amen.

III.

Prayer after Sermon.

ALMIGHTY God, our Lord and Master, the Father of mercy and the God of all comfort, we humbly present to Thee the sacrifice of a thankful spirit, joyfully acknowledging Thine infinite goodness in sending to us the dayspring from on high to enlighten our darkness, and guide our feet into the way of peace. We praise Thy name for that portion of Thy holy Word of which Thou hast made us partakers this day. Grant that it may bring forth fruit unto holiness in our whole life, to the glory of Thy name, the edification of our brethren, and the comfort of our souls in the day of our Lord Jesus Christ.

Here may be introduced any special Prayers, as occasion may require.

Intercessions.

Almighty and ever-living God, we draw near in the name of Thy Son Jesus Christ, our High Priest and Mediator, who hath passed into the heavens, where He abideth at Thy right hand, and ever liveth to make intercession for us. We bring unto Thee the supplications of Thy people, and the prayers of Thy Church: and we beseech Thee that they may come up with acceptance as incense upon Thine altar, and that Thou wilt be favourable unto us, and answer us in peace.

Almighty and everlasting God, we are taught by Thy holy Word that the hearts of kings are in Thy rule and governance, and that Thou dost dispose and turn them as it seemeth best to Thy godly wisdom; we therefore humbly beseech Thee so to dispose and govern the heart of Victoria, our Queen and Governor, that in all her thoughts, words, and works, she may ever seek Thine honour and glory, and study to preserve Thy people committed to her charge, in wealth, peace, and godliness. Grant this, O merciful Father, for Thy dear Son's sake.

We pray also for Albert Edward Prince of Wales, the Princess of Wales, and all the Royal Family.

May Thy spirit instruct and guide the Queen's

counsellors and ministers, and all that are in authority.

Holy Father, keep through Thine own name those whom Thou hast chosen in Christ Jesus; preserve them from the evil that is in the world; sanctify them through Thy truth; let Thy love be manifested in them; fill them with Thy Holy Spirit, that they may be one in Thee, O Father, and in Jesus Christ Thy Son; perfect them in the hope of His coming; give unto them a full entrance into His eternal kingdom, and make them partakers of His glory.

Give unto all nations, we beseech Thee, peace one with another; take away all ambition and wicked lusts, and all that would endanger or destroy godly concord; save us from bloodshed and confusion, and vouchsafe unto all Christian people to dwell together as brethren, in unity and peace.

Stir up the hearts of Christian parents to bring up their children in the nurture and admonition of the Lord. May the young be in such wise prepared to fulfil their calling in this life, that they may adorn the doctrine of their God and Saviour in all things.

Send forth the news of Thy salvation unto the ends of the earth; and turn the hearts of all men, and fetch all Thine erring children home unto Thy fold.

We pray Thee for favourable weather, and

that Thou wilt give us the fruits of the earth in due season.

We beseech Thee for all who are in trouble, sorrow, need, sickness, or any other adversity.

We commend unto Thee all departing this life, and we beseech Thee to receive them to Thy rest.

O Lord, govern us, we beseech Thee, by Thine own almighty power in all things; be Thou long-suffering with all of us, and turn unto us according to our supplications; remember us in Thy tenderness and Thy mercy; visit us in Thy goodness; help us by Thy blessing to escape, through the remainder of this day, the manifold wiles of the wicked one; and preserve our life from all snares by the grace of Thy most Holy Spirit; granting unto us to see the morning and the day in joy, that we may direct our morning prayers unto Thee; through Jesus Christ our Lord.

And unto Thee the Father, with the Son and the Holy Ghost, be all glory and praise, world without end.

Amen.

The Benediction.

The grace of the Lord Jesus Christ, and the love of God, and the communion of the Holy Ghost, be with you all.

Amen.

Fourth Sunday of the Month.

Morning Service.

THE sacrifices of God are a broken spirit; a broken and a contrite heart, O God, Thou wilt not despise.

Offer the sacrifices of righteousness, and put your trust in the Lord.

I.

Prayer of Invocation.

O GOD, the Father of our Lord and Saviour Jesus Christ, the mighty God who art blessed for evermore, we Thy people and the sheep of Thy pasture, draw near to Thee with reverence and godly fear.

Look down from heaven, in Thy tender love, on us approaching Thee through Thy Christ, and sanctify our souls and bodies by Thy Holy Spirit, and strengthen our infirmity, that our prayers may go up before Thee as incense, and be accepted as a sweet savour, through the same Jesus Christ our Lord.

The Confession.

If we say we have no sin, we deceive ourselves, and the truth is not in us. If we confess our sins, Thou art faithful and just to forgive us our sins, and to cleanse us from all unrighteousness.

O most merciful Father, we acknowledge and confess that we have sinned against heaven and in Thy sight, and are not worthy to be called Thy children. We have all gone astray from Thy way like lost sheep, and have walked in counsels of our own. We have known to do good, but we have not done it; we have named the name of Christ, but have not departed from iniquity. Our sins are more in number than the hairs of our head; and we are indebted ten thousand talents, and are unable to pay.

But, O Lord, we repent, and are sorry for our sins. We especially bewail before Thee those things which are the present burden of our hearts and consciences. We cannot stand before Thee as our Judge, but we flee to Thee as our Saviour, hoping in Thy mercies, which are more than can be numbered.

Forsake us not, O God, who put our trust in Thee. Remember not against us former transgressions, but remember Thy loving-kindnesses which have been ever of old. And as Thou wast ever merciful to Thy people Israel, as often as they in penitence turned unto Thee, so do Thou show the like mercy unto us, with whom Thou hast made a better covenant, confirmed and sealed with the blood of Thy beloved Son.

For Pardon and Peace.

Blessed be Thy name, O Lord, that Thou dost, through the ordinances of Thy Church, seal and make sure to Thy people the remission of their sins; wherefore we beseech Thee to grant to all of us who truly repent, and are resolved to walk in newness of life, the comfortable assurance that our transgressions are forgiven, and the peace that cometh from above.

Supplications.

Give ear, O Lord, unto our prayer, and attend to the voice of our supplication.

Pardoned through Christ, and risen with Him, may we have our affections set upon things above, and overcome the world with the victory of faith.

Take away from us, we beseech Thee, whatever is depraved and perverse, whatever is contrary to salvation, whatever is hurtful to the soul, and whatever is displeasing to Thee.

From the lust of the flesh, the lust of the eye, and the pride of life, good Lord, deliver us; and strengthen us, by the grace of the Holy Spirit, to fight the good fight of the faith, to endure hardness as good soldiers of Jesus Christ, to rule our bodies by temperance and our spirits by meekness, and to glorify Thee both with body and spirit which Thou hast redeemed.

O Thou great Master and Lord, whose are all things in heaven and earth, and who givest to every one as it seemeth good in Thy sight; grant us grace so to use the talents which Thou hast committed to us for a season, that when the Lord shall return to reckon with His servants, we may be enabled to give in our account with joy, and not with grief.

O Almighty God, whose eternal providence is over all Thy works, we beseech Thee to help and deliver us Thy servants in all time of our tribulation and adversity, and also in all time of our prosperity and wealth, that we be not overwhelmed with despondency and fear, or lifted up with presumption and pride; but enjoying Thy bounties with humility and thankfulness, and bearing Thy chastening with faith and hope, we may endure unto the end; and having finished the work Thou hast given us to do, may, through Thy mercy, enter into the joy of our Lord.

Here may be introduced any other subject for Supplication.

O God, who hast chosen Zion as Thy rest for ever, and hast promised abundantly to bless her provision, and satisfy her poor with bread, to clothe her priests with salvation, and to cause her saints to shout aloud for joy; grant that, through the ordinances of Thy Church, we may receive out of Christ's fulness, and grace for grace; and being thus nourished by Thy Word and sacraments, may be built up unto everlasting life.

These our humble supplications we offer up to Thee through Thine only begotten Son; and to Thee we ascribe glory, honour, and might, to the Father, and to the Son, and to the Holy Ghost, now and ever, world without end.

Amen.

II.

The Thanksgiving.

O LORD, open Thou our lips; and our mouth shall show forth Thy praise.

Almighty God, Father of mercies, and Giver

of all good, we render thanks unto Thy great name for Thy loving-kindness and tender mercy towards us and all mankind.

We praise Thee for the succession of day and night, summer and winter, seed-time and harvest, and that Thou hast never left Thyself without witness among men, but hast done good to all, sending rain from heaven and fruitful seasons, and filling men's hearts with food and gladness. We thank Thee for our being, our reason, our health, our friends, our food and raiment, for Thy care over us from day to day; for that Thou hast been ever with us through the past time of our lives, and hast brought us safely to this hour.

Here may be introduced any other subject for Thanksgiving.

Above all, with Thy whole Church throughout the world, we adore Thine unfathomable love in the redemption of mankind by our Lord Jesus Christ; for whom and by whom we humbly offer unto Thee most hearty thanks and praise.

We bless Thee for the descent of the Holy Ghost, and for Thy Church filled with His presence; for our baptism and Christian instruction, and for the great hope of everlasting life.

For all these things glory be to Thee, O Lord

God Almighty; blessed be the name of the Lord for ever and ever.

For Illumination.

O God, who didst speak in times past unto the fathers by the prophets, and hast in these last days spoken to us by Thy Son from heaven; give us, we pray Thee, humble, teachable, and obedient hearts, that we may receive what He hath revealed, and do alway what He hath commanded. And as man liveth not by bread alone, but by every word of God, grant that we may ever hunger after this heavenly food, that it may be to us sweeter than honey, and more to be desired than gold, and that we may find in it daily provision on our way to eternal life.

The Lord's Prayer.

Our Father which art in heaven, Hallowed be Thy name. Thy kingdom come. Thy will be done in earth, as it is in heaven. Give us this day our daily bread. And forgive us our trespasses, as we forgive them that trespass against us. And lead us not into temptation; but deliver us from evil: For Thine is the kingdom, and the power, and the glory for ever and ever.
Amen.

III.

Prayer after Sermon.

O LORD our God, with whom is the fulness of salvation, bless to us our meditations on Thy holy Word, and grant that, like a fruitful tree planted by the rivers of Thy grace, we may bring forth fruit here, and may be crowned with glory hereafter.

Here may be introduced any special Prayers, as occasion may require.

Intercessions.

O God, who hast taught us to make supplications, prayers, intercessions, and giving of thanks for all men, we humbly beseech Thee to receive these our prayers which we offer to Thy divine majesty.

We pray for her most sacred Majesty Queen Victoria, that Thou wouldst grant her a long and happy life, faithful counsellors, loyal subjects, a prosperous reign, and finally bestow upon her a crown of glory.

We pray for Albert Edward Prince of Wales, the Princess of Wales, and all the Royal Family, that Thou wouldst regard them with Thy favour, and so dispose their hearts that they may be nursing-fathers and nursing-mothers to the Church.

We pray [for the High Court of Parliament] for the nobles, rulers, judges, and magistrates of the land, [and for the magistrates of this town], that Thou wouldst inspire them with Thy wisdom and grant them Thy blessing.

We pray for the Army and Navy, that they may be distinguished by loyalty and valour, temperance and godliness.

We pray for the United Kingdom, with all its colonies and dependencies, beseeching Thee to preserve our peace and defend our liberties, to prosper our trade and commerce, to send healthful and seasonable weather, to bless our husbandry, and to crown the year with Thy goodness.

Almighty God, who hast made of one blood all nations, we pray for the peace of the whole world, and the salvation of all men. Look in pity upon Thine ancient people, whose are the fathers, and of whom according to the flesh Jesus Christ our Lord and Saviour came; and have mercy upon all who are in bondage to heathen superstition, and fetch them home, blessed Lord, to Thy flock, that they may be saved among the remnant of the true Israelites.

We pray especially for the good estate of the Catholic Church; that the divisions which desolate Thine heritage may be healed; that what is wanting anywhere may be supplied; and that every plant that is not of Thy planting may be rooted up.

We pray for all pastors and ministers of Thy Word, [and particularly for him [those] to whom Thou hast given the charge of this flock], that they may take heed to themselves and to all the flocks over which the Holy Ghost hath made them overseers, to feed the Church of Christ which He hath purchased with His blood, that when the chief Shepherd shall appear, they may receive a crown of glory that fadeth not away.

We pray for this parish, that those among us who bear office may be ensamples to the flock; that the young may abide in Christ, into whom they have been engrafted, and be spared for lives of piety and usefulness; that the middle-aged may be strong for the Lord and valiant for the right; and that those advanced in years may have bodily comfort, and joy in the Holy Ghost, and finally a good end, and an abundant entrance into rest.

We pray for the poor and needy, the desolate and the oppressed, the widow and the orphan, the weak and the bowed down; beseeching Thee to remember them in mercy, and to visit them in Thy compassion.

We pray for those who mourn, that they may be comforted; for those who suffer pain and anguish, that they may be relieved; for those in sickness, that they may be healed, and may again praise Thee in the sanctuary [and for any such known to ourselves whom we name in our hearts before Thee]; and especially we commend to Thee the dying, entreating Thee to be with them in that last hour when heart and flesh do faint and fail, to cleanse their souls in the blood of Christ, and to receive them into Thy rest.

O Thou who art the confidence of the ends of the earth, and of them that are far off upon the sea, we commend to Thy almighty protection all travellers, sojourners, and strangers. Journey with them who journey, and grant to them who are far from their homes that they may revisit them, in Thy good time, in peace.

O Thou who art the God of all the families of the earth, we beseech Thee to bless all our friends and kindred, and to grant that we may ever be knit together in the bonds of mutual love, and, above all, that we may be members together of the mystical body of Christ.

And O God, our heavenly Father, with whom do live the spirits of the just made perfect, we give Thee thanks for all near and dear to us who have been washed from their sins in the blood of the Lamb, and who, having accomplished their warfare, are at rest with Thee.

Finally, O Lord, we pray for each other, all for each, that Thou wouldst bless us outwardly in our bodies, inwardly in our souls, and grant us good success in all our labours. That which is good and profitable do Thou supply unto us. Give us the peace that cometh from above, and also peace in this world. Grant that we may spend the remainder of this day in Thy fear; and may Thy goodness and mercy follow us all our days, and may we dwell in Thy house for evermore.

Amen.

The Benediction.

The grace of the Lord Jesus Christ, and the love of God, and the communion of the Holy Ghost, be with you all.

Amen.

Evening Service.

THERE be many that say, Who will show us any good? Lord, lift Thou up the light of Thy countenance upon us.

Give ear to our words, O Lord; consider our meditation. Hearken unto the voice of our cry, our King, and our God; for unto Thee will we pray.

I.

Prayer of Invocation.

O ALMIGHTY God, from whom cometh down every good and perfect gift; pour out upon us the spirit of grace and supplications; deliver us from coldness of heart and wanderings of mind, that, with steadfast thoughts and kindled affections, we may worship Thee in spirit and in truth; through Jesus Christ our Lord.

The Confession.

Hear, O Lord, the humble confession of our sin.

We confess unto Thee, Father Almighty,

Lord of heaven and earth, our sins which we have committed against Thee, and against the law of Christ. We confess unto Thee the wickedness of our hearts, out of which have proceeded all manner of evil thoughts and acts, for which things' sake Thy wrath is kindled against us, and we are without excuse before Thee this day. But especially, O God, we bewail those things which are the present burden of our heart and conscience. For all our sins and transgressions, our iniquities and offences, which Thou bringest to our remembrance, we cast ourselves upon Thy mercy; and those which, through ignorance or carelessness, through foolishness, or the sinful darkness of our heart, we remember not, but which Thou, who knowest all secrets, seest that we have committed against Thee, do Thou forgive; and do Thou cleanse us from them all, for Thy mercy's sake, O Lord. And accept our confession, and make our repentance sincere, through Jesus Christ.

For Pardon and Peace.

As the heaven is high above the earth, so great is Thy mercy toward them that fear Thee.

Who is a God like unto Thee, who pardonest iniquity, and retainest not Thine anger for ever; because Thou delightest in mercy?

We rejoice in Thy promises, O God: we hope in Thy Word. Being justified freely by Thy grace, may we be made heirs, according to the hope of everlasting life. And having this hope in us, may we cleanse ourselves from all filthiness both of the flesh and of the spirit, and perfect holiness in Thy fear; that the peace of God, which passeth all understanding, may keep our hearts and minds through Christ Jesus.

Supplications.

Hear, O Lord, our humble supplications. Give us so to know Christ and His life, that the same mind which was in Him may be in us; that we may be in the world as He was in the world.

Give us so to know Christ and His death, that we may not glory save in His cross; whereby the world is crucified unto us, and we unto the world.

Give us so to know Christ and the power of His resurrection, that like as He was raised from the dead by the glory of the Father, we also may walk in newness of life.

Give us so to know Christ and His ascension, that our conversation may be in heaven; and that we may seek those things that are above, where He sitteth at Thy right hand.

Give us so to know Christ and His second

coming, that our lamps may be burning and our loins girt, and we ourselves as servants waiting for their master.

Give us so to know Christ as Judge of quick and of dead, that we may give in our account with joy, and may be welcomed by Him to the kingdom of the Father.

May we live by faith in Christ; may we increase in union with Him; may we every day become more and more like Him, till we see Him as He is, and be changed into His perfect likeness.

Grant that without terror we may await His peaceful coming; that He may find us not sleeping in our sins, but awake and rejoicing in His praises: that we may go forth undefiled to meet Him in the company of His saints, and may be found worthy of the banquet of eternal life.

Here may be introduced any other subject for Supplication.

O God, all righteous and all holy, regard not, we beseech Thee, the infirmities by which our prayers are marred, but in Thy mercy accept them, for the sake of Him who is the only propitiation for mankind. Let the cry of Thy family enter into Thine ears, O Father, and send unto Thy children an answer in peace; through our Elder Brother Jesus Christ, who is also our High Priest and Sacrifice, and the Altar which sanctifieth our gift; and to whom, with Thee and the Holy Ghost, be all glory in the Church, for ever and ever.

Amen.

II.

The Thanksgiving.

O GOD, according to Thy name, so is Thy praise unto the ends of the earth.

In goodness art Thou exalted, O Lord our Father, for ever and for ever. We magnify Thee, we praise Thee, we worship Thee; we give thanks unto Thee for Thy bountiful providence, for all the blessings of the present life, and all the hopes of a better life to come. Let the memory of Thy goodness, we beseech Thee, fill our hearts with joy and thankfulness unto our life's end; and let no unworthiness of ours provoke Thee to withhold from us any needed good, seeing that all Thy blessings come not by our desert, but only through the merit and mediation of Jesus Christ our Lord.

Here may be introduced any other subject for Thanksgiving.

For Illumination.

God of all peace and consolation, who didst gloriously fulfil the great promise of the Gospel by sending down the Holy Ghost on the day of Pentecost, to establish the Church as the house of His continual presence and power among men; mercifully grant unto us, we beseech Thee, this same gift of the Spirit to renew, illuminate, refresh, and sanctify our souls; to be over us and around us like the light and dew of heaven, and to be in us evermore as a well of water springing up into everlasting life; through Jesus Christ our Lord.

The Lord's Prayer.

Our Father which art in heaven, Hallowed be Thy name. Thy kingdom come. Thy will be done in earth, as it is in heaven. Give us this day our daily bread. And forgive us our trespasses, as we forgive them that trespass against us. And lead us not into temptation; but deliver us from evil: For Thine is the kingdom, and the power, and the glory for ever and ever. Amen.

III.

Prayer after Sermon.

Almighty God, who hast builded Thy Church upon the foundation of the apostles and prophets, Jesus Christ Himself being the chief corner-stone; grant that, being illuminated through the words of Thy prophets, and joined together in unity of spirit through the doctrine, precepts, and ministry of Thine apostles, we may grow unto a holy temple in the Lord, and may be builded together for Thy habitation, through the Spirit.

Here may be introduced any special Prayers, as occasion may require.

Intercessions.

O God of infinite mercy, who hast compassion on all men, and relievest the necessities of all that call to Thee for help; hear the prayers of Thy servants when they cry unto Thee, and send them help from Thy holy habitation.

Regard with the favour which Thou bearest unto Thine anointed her most sacred Majesty the Queen; preserve her in health, honour, and prosperity. In her days may the righteous flourish, and may there be abundance of peace. And after she has done Thy will upon the earth, do Thou crown her with glory, honour, and immortality.

Bless, we beseech Thee, Albert Edward Prince of Wales, the Princess of Wales, and all the members of the Royal House.

Let Thy mercy descend upon the whole Church; preserve her in truth and peace, in unity and safety, amidst all troubles, and against all temptations and enemies; that she, offering to Thee the never-ceasing sacrifice of prayer and thanksgiving, may advance the honour of her Lord, and be filled with His Spirit, and partake of His glory.

Remember them that minister in holy things; let Thy priests be clothed with righteousness, and let Thy saints shout for joy.

Be pleased, O Lord, to remember our friends and benefactors; do Thou good to them, and return all their kindness double into their own bosom; rewarding them with blessings, sanctifying them with Thy grace, and bringing them to Thine eternal kingdom.

Let all our families, and kindred, and neighbours, receive the benefit of our prayers and the blessing of the Most High, the comforts and the supports of Thy providence, and the sanctification of Thy Spirit.

Relieve and comfort all the persecuted and

afflicted; speak peace to troubled consciences; strengthen the weak; confirm the strong; instruct the ignorant; deliver the oppressed from him that spoileth him, and relieve the needy, and him that hath no helper; and bring us all, by the waters of comfort and in the ways of righteousness, to Thy kingdom of rest and glory; through Jesus Christ our Lord.

These things we ask, O heavenly Father, in patient confidence and joyful hope, being assured that we ask them according to Thy will, that the voice of Thy Church is heard by Thee, that the intercessions of the Holy Ghost are known unto Thee, and that the mediation of Thy well-beloved Son, our Lord and Saviour, doth prevail with Thee.

And unto Thee, the Father, with Thy Son and with the Holy Ghost, be all glory, as it was in the beginning, is now, and ever shall be, world without end.

Amen.

The Benediction.

The grace of the Lord Jesus Christ, and the love of God, and the communion of the Holy Ghost, be with you all.

Amen.

Fifth Sunday of the Month.

Morning Service.

WE will come into Thy house in the multitude of Thy mercy; and in Thy fear will we worship toward Thy holy temple.

Let the words of our mouth, and the meditation of our heart, be acceptable in Thy sight, O Lord, our strength and our Redeemer.

I.

Prayer of Invocation.

O GOD, most High and Holy, who dwellest in the holy place, make us holy, and bring us near to Thee, and cleanse us from all defilement, that we may perform the worship of our fathers in Thy fear, for Thou art He that blesseth and halloweth all things; through Jesus Christ our Lord.

The Confession.

If we say that we have no sin, we deceive ourselves, and the truth is not in us. If we confess our sins, Thou art faithful and just to forgive us our sins, and to cleanse us from all unrighteousness.

O God, searcher of hearts, in whom there is no darkness, and from whom our sins cannot be covered, we humble ourselves before Thy holy majesty; we confess that we have been foolish, rebellious, deceived. We have been unthankful for Thy mercies, distrustful of Thy promises, disobedient to Thy commands, and by our manifold wickedness have provoked Thee to cast us off from Thy favour and fellowship. Behold, we return unto Thee our God, from whose ways we have so grievously departed, and implore Thy pardon for all our sin and folly. Forgive us, we beseech Thee; forgive Thy people, whom Thou hast redeemed with the most precious blood of Thy dear Son; create in us clean and contrite hearts, and vouchsafe unto us Thy heavenly grace, that we turn not again unto folly; and give unto us heartily to forgive others, as we beseech Thee to forgive us, and to serve Thee henceforth in newness of life, to the glory of Thy holy name; through Jesus Christ our Lord.

For Pardon and Peace.

O Lord, we beseech Thee mercifully to regard us, and spare all them that have confessed their faults unto Thee; that they whose consciences by sin are accused, by Thy merciful pardon may now be absolved; through Jesus Christ our Lord.

Supplications.

Give ear, O Lord, unto our prayer, and attend to the voice of our supplication.

O Lord, make us poor in spirit: that ours may be the kingdom of heaven.

Make us to mourn for sin: that we may be comforted by Thy grace.

Make us meek, O Lord: that we may inherit the earth.

Make us to hunger and thirst after righteousness: that we may be filled therewith.

Make us merciful, O Lord: that we may obtain mercy.

Make us pure in heart: that we may see Thee our God.

Make us peacemakers: that we may be called Thy children.

Make us willing to be persecuted for righteousness' sake: that our reward may be great in heaven.

O God, true and highest Life, by whom, through whom, and in whom, all things live, which live truly and blessedly; pity and help us, according as Thou knowest we need, in body and in soul, that being freed from the chains with which we are bound, and casting off all that entangles us, we may serve and cleave to Thee alone, who knowest all things, and canst perform all things, and who livest for evermore.

Here may be introduced any other subject for Supplication.

Hasten, we entreat Thee, O Lord, the second and glorious appearing of Thy Son, our Saviour Jesus Christ; and grant unto us that, daily looking for that blessed hope, we may not sleep as do others, but may watch and be sober, exercising ourselves unto godliness, and working out our own salvation with fear and trembling; that we, with all Thy saints, may be presented holy and unblameable before the presence of Thy glory with exceeding joy; through Him that loved us, and washed us from our sins in His own blood.

Give ear, O God, unto our prayers, and grant unto us the light of Thy grace here, and the light of Thy glory hereafter; through Jesus Christ our Lord.

Amen.

II.

The Thanksgiving.

O LORD, open Thou our lips; and our mouth shall show forth Thy praise.

We render thanks unto Thy name, O God, most high; for Thou hast created us in Thine own image; Thou hast given us souls to know and love Thee; Thou hast made us but a little lower than the angels; Thou hast supplied all our wants; Thou hast loaded us with Thy benefits; Thou hast caused our cup to run over.

Here may be introduced any other subject for Thanksgiving.

We have sinned against Thee, but Thou hast spared us; we have wandered from Thee, but Thou hast sought us; we were lost, but Thou hast saved us. O God our Saviour, Thou hast broken our chains, that we might be free; Thou hast healed our diseased souls, that we might not perish: Thou hast enriched us who were poor with the treasures of Thy salvation; Thou hast made us who had nothing to inherit all things; and even now, all things are ours. Therefore, with one heart and with one voice we laud and magnify Thy glorious name; and, with Thy saints on earth and in heaven, we ascribe blessing, and honour, and glory, and power, unto Him that sitteth upon the throne, and unto the Lamb, for ever and for ever.

For Illumination.

O God, whose Word is quick and powerful, and sharper than a two-edged sword, grant unto us who are here before Thee that we may receive Thy truth into our hearts, in faith and love. By it may we be taught and guided, upheld and comforted; that we be no longer children in understanding, but grow to the stature of perfect men in Christ and be prepared to every good word and work, to the honour of Thy name; through Jesus Christ our Lord.

The Lord's Prayer.

Our Father which art in heaven, Hallowed be Thy name. Thy kingdom come. Thy will be done in earth, as it is in heaven. Give us this day our daily bread. And forgive us our trespasses, as we forgive them that trespass against us. And lead us not into temptation; but deliver us from evil: For Thine is the kingdom, and the power, and the glory for ever and ever.
Amen.

III.

Prayer after Sermon.

O GOD, who hast revealed to us the light of Thy Gospel, and called us into the fellowship of Thy Son Jesus Christ, bless to us Thy Word which we have heard this day; and grant that we may put away the works of darkness, and may walk in purity, uprightness, and sincerity; that we may have fellowship with Thee, for Thou art light, and with Thee there is no darkness at all; that, when the shadows of this mortal life are passed away, we may behold those things which eye hath not seen, and be made partakers of everlasting glory; through Jesus Christ our Lord.

Here may be introduced any special Prayers, as occasion may require.

Intercessions.

O God, who hast taught us by Thy holy apostle that we should make supplications, prayers, intercessions, and giving of thanks for all men, we humbly beseech Thee to receive these our prayers, which we offer to Thy divine majesty.

Remember, we beseech Thee, every creature

of Thine for good, and visit the whole world with Thy mercy.

O Thou Preserver and Lord of men, look graciously upon mankind; and as Thou hast concluded all under sin and unbelief, so let Thy pity and Thy pardon extend unto all.

O Thou great King of all the earth, preserve, we beseech Thee, all Christian princes, more especially her most sacred Majesty Queen Victoria, Albert Edward Prince of Wales, the Princess of Wales, and all the members of the Royal Family; that, being faithful servants of Thee, the King of kings, they may inherit the crown of everlasting glory.

O Thou who distributest among men degrees of power severally as Thou wilt, grant that all persons of eminence and authority may be eminent for virtue and sincere regard to Thy holy faith. Fill them with all godly wisdom; guide them in the administration of justice to all persons and in all causes; and give all Thy people grace to live in subjection to them, not only for wrath, but also for conscience' sake. Bless, we beseech Thee [the High Court of Parliament now assembled, and] all rulers, judges, and magistrates, [especially the magistrates of this town.]

O Thou who art the wholesome defence and strength of Thine Anointed, bless, we beseech Thee, Thy Holy Catholic Church; remove all her divisions; root out of her all heresies and false doctrines; let her live by Thy Spirit, and reign in Thy glory; bring back to the fold those who have erred and strayed therefrom; and grant that all who confess Thy holy name may agree in the truth of Thy holy Word, and live in unity and godly concord.

O Thou who art the reward of them that wait upon Thee, send down a double portion of Thy Spirit upon those whom Thou hast set apart to minister in holy things; [particularly him [those] to whom Thou hast given the charge of this flock;] that they may do it with clean hands and pure hearts; that they may be guides to the blind, comforters to the weary and heavy-laden; that they may strengthen the weak and confirm the strong; that they may boldly rebuke sin, and patiently suffer for the truth.

O Thou Lord of the harvest, send forth, we pray Thee, labourers fitted to do the work of that harvest. Let the Sun of Righteousness give light to those who sit in darkness. Let Thy Gospel have free course and be glorified.

O Thou Helper of the helpless, our seasonable refuge in the time of trouble, remember all who are in any sort of extremity, and who call upon Thee for succour and protection; relieve their necessities, and lighten their burdens; give them patience and submission to Thy blessed will, and in Thy due time deliver them from all their troubles.

Especially we commend into Thy merciful hands the souls of Thy servants departing from the body, most humbly beseeching Thee that they may be precious in Thy sight. Receive them into the blessed arms of Thine unspeakable mercy, into the sacred rest of everlasting peace, and into the glorious estate of Thy chosen saints in heaven.

Finally, O Lord, we commit to Thy keeping and protection, now, henceforth, and for ever, our souls and bodies, our minds and thoughts, our prayers and desires, our life and death, our kindred and our friends, those who have asked us to pray for them, and all those for whom we ought ourselves specially to pray [and for any such known to ourselves, whom we name in our hearts before Thee]. God the Father, preserve and keep us; God the Son, assist and strengthen us; God the Holy Ghost, defend and aid us; God the Holy Trinity, be ever with us. Let Thy merciful kindness be upon us, even as we do put our trust in Thee.

Amen.

The Benediction.

The grace of the Lord Jesus Christ, and the love of God, and the communion of the Holy Ghost, be with you all.

Amen.

Evening Service.

WHEN the wicked man turneth away from his wickedness that he hath committed, and doeth that which is lawful and right, he shall save his soul alive.

Enter not into judgment with Thy servants, O Lord; for in Thy sight shall no man living be justified.

I.

Prayer of Invocation.

ALMIGHTY God, unto whom all hearts be open, all desires known, and from whom no secrets are hid, cleanse the thoughts of our hearts by the inspiration of Thy Holy Spirit, that we may perfectly love Thee, and worthily magnify Thy holy name; through Christ our Lord.

The Confession.

Almighty and most merciful Father, we have erred and strayed from Thy ways like lost sheep. We have followed too much the devices and desires of our own hearts. We have offended against Thy holy laws. We have left undone those things which we ought to have done, and we have done those things which we ought not to have done; and there is no health in us. But Thou, O Lord, have mercy upon us, miserable offenders. Spare Thou them, O God, which confess their faults. Restore Thou them that are penitent; according to Thy promises declared unto mankind in Christ Jesus our Lord. And grant, O most merciful Father, for His sake, that we may hereafter live a godly, righteous, and sober life, to the glory of Thy holy name.

For Pardon and Peace.

Almighty God, the Father of our Lord Jesus Christ, who desirest not the death of a sinner, but rather that he may turn from his wickedness and live; and who pardonest and absolvest all them that truly repent, and unfeignedly believe Thy holy Gospel; grant us, we beseech Thee, true repentance and Thy Holy Spirit, that those things may please Thee which we do at this present; and that the rest of our life hereafter may be pure and holy, so that at the last we may come to Thine eternal joy; through Jesus Christ our Lord.

Supplications.

Almighty Father, who hast given Thine only Son to die for our sins, and to rise again for our justification, grant us so to put away the leaven of malice and wickedness, that we may alway serve Thee in pureness of living and truth; through the merits of the same, Thy Son, Jesus Christ our Lord.

O Lord, who hast taught us that all our doings without charity are nothing worth, send Thy Holy Ghost, and pour into our hearts that most excellent gift of charity, the very bond of peace, and of all virtues, without which whosoever liveth is counted dead before Thee; grant this for Thine only Son Jesus Christ's sake.

Almighty God, who seest that we have no power of ourselves to help ourselves, keep us both outwardly in our bodies, and inwardly in our souls, that we may be defended from all adversities which may happen to the body, and from all evil thoughts which may assault and hurt the soul; through Jesus Christ our Lord.

O God, from whom all holy desires, all good counsels, and all just works do proceed, give unto Thy servants that peace which the world cannot give; that both our hearts may be set to obey Thy commandments, and also that by Thee, we, being defended from the fear of our enemies, may pass our time in rest and quietness; through the merits of Jesus Christ our Saviour.

Here may be introduced any other subject for Supplication.

O God, whose blessed Son was manifested, that He might destroy the works of the devil, and make us the sons of God and heirs of eternal life, grant us, we beseech Thee, that, having this hope, we may purify ourselves, even as He is pure; that when He shall appear again with power and great glory, we may be made like unto Him in His eternal and glorious kingdom: where with Thee, O Father, and Thee, O Holy Ghost, He liveth and reigneth, ever one God, world without end.
Amen.

II.

The Thanksgiving.

ALMIGHTY God, Father of all mercies, we Thine unworthy servants do give Thee most humble and hearty thanks for all Thy goodness and loving-kindness to us, and to all men [particularly to those who desire now to offer up their praises and thanksgivings for Thy late mercies vouchsafed unto them].

Here may be introduced any special subject for Thanksgiving.

We bless Thee for our creation, preservation, and all the blessings of this life; but above all, for Thine inestimable love, in the redemption of the world by our Lord Jesus Christ, for the means of grace, and for the hope of glory. And, we beseech Thee, give us that due sense of all Thy mercies, that our hearts may be unfeignedly thankful, and that we show forth Thy praise, not only with our lips, but in our lives; by giving up ourselves to Thy service, and by walking before Thee in holiness and righteousness all our days; through Jesus Christ our Lord: to whom, with Thee and the Holy Ghost, be all honour and glory, world without end.

For Illumination.

O Lord Jesus Christ, who at Thy first coming didst send Thy messenger to prepare the way before Thee, grant that the ministers and stewards of Thy mysteries may likewise so prepare and make ready Thy way, by turning the hearts of the disobedient to the wisdom of the just, that at Thy second coming to judge the world we may be found an acceptable people in Thy sight, who livest and reignest with the Father and the Holy Ghost, ever one God, world without end.

The Lord's Prayer.

Our Father which art in heaven, Hallowed be Thy name. Thy kingdom come. Thy will be done in earth, as it is in heaven. Give us this day our daily bread. And forgive us our trespasses, as we forgive them that trespass against us. And lead us not into temptation; but deliver us from evil: For Thine is the kingdom, and the power, and the glory, for ever and ever.

Amen.

III.

Prayer after Sermon.

GRANT, we beseech Thee, Almighty God, that the words which we have heard this day with our outward ears, may through Thy grace be so grafted inwardly in our hearts, that they may bring forth in us the fruit of good living, to the honour and praise of Thy name; through Jesus Christ our Lord.

Prevent us, O Lord, in all our doings, with Thy most gracious favour, and further us with Thy continual help; that in all our works begun, continued, and ended in Thee, we may glorify Thy holy name, and finally by Thy mercy obtain everlasting life; through Jesus Christ our Lord.

Here may be introduced any special Prayers, as occasion may require.

Intercessions.

Almighty and ever-living God, who by Thy holy apostle hast taught us to make prayers and supplications, and to give thanks, for all men, we humbly beseech Thee most mercifully to receive these our prayers, which we offer unto Thy divine majesty; beseeching Thee to inspire continually the universal Church with the spirit of truth, unity, and concord. And grant that all they that do confess Thy holy name may agree in the truth of Thy holy Word, and live in unity and godly love.

We beseech Thee also to save and defend all Christian kings, princes, and governors; and specially Thy servant Victoria, our Queen; that under her we may be godly and quietly governed. And grant unto her whole Council, and to all that are put in authority under her, that they may truly and impartially minister justice, to the punishment of wickedness and vice, and to the maintenance of Thy true religion and virtue.

Give grace, O heavenly Father, to all pastors and ministers, that they may both by their life and doctrine set forth Thy true and lively Word, and rightly and duly administer Thy holy sacraments: and to all Thy people give Thy heavenly grace; and especially to this congregation here present, that, with meek heart and due reverence, they may hear and receive Thy holy Word, truly serving Thee in holiness and righteousness all the days of their life.

And we most humbly beseech Thee of Thy goodness, O Lord, to comfort and succour all them who in this transitory life are in trouble, sorrow, need, sickness, or any other adversity. And we also bless Thy holy name for all Thy servants departed this life in Thy faith and fear; beseeching Thee to give us grace so to follow their good examples, that with them we may be partakers of Thy heavenly kingdom. Grant this, O Father, for Jesus Christ's sake, our only Mediator and Advocate.

Lighten our darkness, we beseech Thee, O Lord, and by Thy great mercy defend us from all snares and dangers of this night; for the love of Thine only Son our Saviour, Jesus Christ.

Almighty God, who hast given us grace at this time with one accord to make our common supplications unto Thee, and dost promise that when two or three are gathered together in Thy name Thou wilt grant their requests; fulfil now, O Lord, the desires and petitions of Thy servants, as may be most expedient for them; granting us in this world knowledge of Thy truth, and in the world to come life everlasting.
Amen.

The Benediction.

The grace of the Lord Jesus Christ, and the love of God, and the communion of the Holy Ghost, be with you all.
Amen.

The Order

for the

Administration of Holy Baptism.

The Minister begins the Service with the following sentence—

OUR help is in the name of the Lord, who made heaven and earth.

And then says—

Dearly beloved, attend to the words of the institution of this Holy Sacrament, as delivered by our Lord and Saviour to His disciples, after His resurrection, and before His ascension to the right hand of God :—

" All power is given unto me in heaven and in earth. Go ye, therefore, and teach all nations, baptizing them in the name of the Father, and of the Son, and of the Holy Ghost; teaching them to observe all things whatsoever I have commanded you: and, lo, I am with you alway, even unto the end of the world."

The Sacrament thus instituted is a sign and seal of our ingrafting into Christ, of remission of sin by His blood, and regeneration by His Spirit, of adoption, and resurrection unto everlasting life; and by it we are solemnly admitted, by Christ's appointment, into His Church, and enter into an engagement to be the Lord's.

And although our young children do not understand these things, they are not to be excluded from this holy ordinance; for consider what is written in the Gospels:—

"And they brought young children unto Him that He should put His hands on them and pray. And His disciples rebuked those that brought them. But when Jesus saw it, He was much displeased, and said, Suffer the little children to come unto me, and forbid them not; for of such is the kingdom of God. Verily I say unto you, Whosoever shall not receive the kingdom of God as a little child, he shall not enter therein. And He took them up in His arms, put His hands upon them, and blessed them."

We read also that on the day of Pentecost, when St Peter called upon the people, saying,

"Repent and be baptized, every one of you, in the name of Jesus Christ, for the remission of sins, and ye shall receive the gift of the Holy Ghost," he assured them that the promise pertained not only to them, but also to their children. And as the Lord thus promiseth to be their God, they are in their Baptism solemnly engaged to be His people.

It is plainly the duty, therefore, of those who dedicate children to God in this Holy Sacrament, to make profession of the faith wherein they are to be baptized; and to promise that they shall be trained up in that faith, and in the fear of the Lord.

Then the Minister says to those who present the child—

You therefore will now make those declarations and promises which are required of you.

Do you hold the Christian Belief, whereof we make confession, saying, I believe in God the Father Almighty, Maker of heaven and earth; and in Jesus Christ His only Son our Lord, who was conceived by the Holy Ghost, born of the Virgin Mary, suffered under Pontius Pilate, was crucified, dead, and buried: He descended into hell; the third day He rose again from the dead; He ascended into heaven, and sitteth on the right hand of God the Father Almighty; from thence He shall come to judge the quick and the dead. I believe in the Holy Ghost; the holy Catholic Church; the communion of saints; the forgiveness of sins; the resurrection of the body; and the life everlasting?

Ans.—We do.

Do you dedicate this child to be baptized in this faith, and to be thereby engaged to renounce the devil, the world, and the flesh; and do you solemnly promise that *he* shall be brought up in the nurture and admonition of the Lord, and in the doctrines and duties of our holy religion?

Ans.—We do.

Or—

Do you present this child to be baptized in the name of the Father, and of the Son, and of the Holy Ghost; and do you promise that *he* shall be brought up in the nurture and admonition of the Lord?

Ans.—We do.

The Minister then says—

The Lord preserve you and the child, and give you grace faithfully to perform these promises.

𝔏et us 𝔓ray.

ALMIGHTY and ever-living God, whose dearly beloved Son, Jesus Christ our Lord, gave commandment to His apostles that they should go teach all nations, and baptize them in the name of the Father, and of the Son, and of the Holy Ghost; we humbly call upon Thee to bless Thine own ordinance now to be administered, and to ratify in heaven what by Thine appointment we do upon earth.

We dedicate this child to Thee, assured that it is not Thy will that one of these little ones should perish. Look mercifully upon *him*, we beseech Thee, that *he* may receive remission of sin, and be born again of water and of the Holy Ghost. May *his* name be enrolled in the Lamb's book of life, never to be blotted out; and *he* being planted into the likeness of the death and resurrection of Christ, may the body of sin be so destroyed in *him* that *he* may serve Thee in newness of life.

Sanctify this water to the spiritual use for which Thou hast ordained it; and grant, we beseech Thee, that this child now to be baptized therein may receive the fulness of Thy grace, and ever remain in the number of Thy faithful children; through Jesus Christ our Lord.

𝔄men.

Then the Parent, or other Sponsor, presenting the child at the font or laver (the Congregation standing), the Minister says—

Name this child.

Ans.—M. [or N.]

Then the Minister, pronouncing the name aloud, pours or sprinkles water upon the child's face, saying—

M. [or N.], I baptize thee in the name of the Father, and of the Son, and of the Holy Ghost.

Amen.

Then the Minister may add—

The grace of the Lord Jesus Christ, and the love of God, and the communion of the Holy Ghost, be with thee.

Amen.

Or—

The Lord bless thee and keep thee. The Lord make His face to shine upon thee, and be gracious unto thee. The Lord lift up His countenance upon thee, and give thee peace.

Amen.

This child is now received, by Christ's appointment, into His Church, and is engaged to confess the faith of Christ crucified, and to continue Christ's faithful soldier and servant unto *his* life's end.

Let us Pray.

WE yield Thee hearty thanks, most merciful Father, that it hath pleased Thee to receive this child into Thy holy Church, to be a partaker of the inestimable benefits purchased by the blood of Thy dear Son; and we beseech Thee to grant that being ingrafted into Christ the true vine, *he* may evermore abide in Him and receive out of His fulness. As the Lord Jesus hath now in this Holy Sacrament taken *him* in His arms and blessed *him*, may *he* with heart and mind embrace Christ as *his* Redeemer, and rejoice in Him as all *his* salvation, and all *his* desire. May *he* grow in wisdom and in stature, and in favour with God and man. Suffer *him* not to fall away from Thee, but may *he* in due time heartily renew *his* baptismal vows; may *he* witness a good confession, and persevering to the end, obtain a full and final victory, through Jesus Christ our Lord.

[Almighty God, by whose blessing mankind is increased, we give Thee thanks on behalf of the parents of this child; and we beseech Thee to grant, that receiving *him* as Thy gift, and being ever mindful of their solemn obligations, they may be diligent and faithful in training *him* up for Thy service and glory. We bless Thee that Thou didst regard the low estate of

Thine handmaiden, and didst send her deliverance in the time of trouble. May the life which Thou hast spared, and the life which Thou hast given, be precious in Thy sight, preserved by Thy care, and devoted to Thy glory. May Thy peace and blessing rest upon these parents and their home, and may this child [their children] be to them a comfort and a blessing].

Sanctify to all of us the administration of this Holy Sacrament. We look back with heartfelt gratitude to our own Baptism, and we bless Thee for the privileges and benefits conferred therein. We have to humble ourselves before Thee for our sinful defilement, our falling short of, and walking contrary to, the grace of Baptism and our solemn vows. We beseech Thee to cleanse us from all our guilt by the blood of Christ, and to grant that henceforth we may have our conversation in holiness and righteousness, and may walk in brotherly love, as being baptized by the same Spirit into one body.

Our Father which art in heaven, Hallowed be Thy name. Thy kingdom come. Thy will be done in earth, as it is in heaven. Give us this day our daily bread. And forgive us our trespasses, as we forgive them that trespass against us. And lead us not into temptation; but deliver us from evil: For Thine is the kingdom, and the power, and the glory, for ever and ever.

Amen.

The grace of the Lord Jesus Christ, and the love of God, and the communion of the Holy Ghost, be with you all.

Amen.

The Order

for the

Admission of Catechumens

to the

Confirmation of the Baptismal Vow,

and to the

Participation of the Lord's Supper.

On the day of preparation for the Lord's Supper, after the sermon, the Minister shall say—

Dearly beloved,—We are now about to admit to the Confirmation of their Baptismal Vow, and to the participation of the Lord's Supper, the catechumens who have been under special instruction in the truths of the Gospel, and who are ready to profess publicly the faith into which they were baptized.

The Minister shall then read their names, and they will come forward and stand in front of the Communion Table.

Addressing the Catechumens, the Minister shall say—

Dearly beloved,—In the days of your infancy you were by Holy Baptism ingrafted into the Lord Jesus Christ, and engaged to be His. God, in His mercy, has spared you to years of responsibility; and you have now, of your own choice, come forward to own and accept, before God and His Church, the covenant then made on your behalf, to profess your faith in the Lord Jesus, to consecrate yourselves to Him, and thereby to bind yourselves anew to His service.

This is one of the most solemn acts in the Christian's life. I charge you, therefore, to answer with all sincerity, and as in the presence of God, who sees your hearts, the questions which I have now to put to you.

Do you receive the doctrine of that holy faith into which you were baptized, whereof we make confession, saying, I believe in God the Father Almighty, Maker of heaven and earth; and in Jesus Christ His only Son our Lord, who was conceived by the Holy Ghost, born of the Virgin Mary, suffered under Pontius Pilate, was crucified, dead, and buried: He descended into hell; the third day he rose again from the dead; He ascended into heaven, and sitteth on

ADMISSION OF CATECHUMENS.

the right hand of God the Father Almighty; from thence He shall come to judge the quick and the dead. I believe in the Holy Ghost; the holy Catholic Church; the communion of saints; the forgiveness of sins; the resurrection of the body; and the life everlasting. These articles of the Christian faith, and the whole doctrine of the Old and New Testaments, you profess to believe: do you not?

Ans.—I do.

Do you ratify and confirm the vow of your baptism, and consecrate yourselves to God as your Father, to Christ as your Saviour, and to the Holy Ghost as your Sanctifier, promising in dependence upon Divine aid to serve the Lord, and keep His commandments all the days of your life?

Ans.—I do.

Do you promise to submit yourselves to all the ordinances of Christ, to use faithfully the means of grace, and to give to the relief of the poor, and the extension of the Church, as the Lord may prosper you?

Ans.—I do.

Then the Minister shall say—

In consequence of these declarations and promises, and being satisfied as to your baptism, your Christian knowledge and life, I do now, in the name of our Lord Jesus Christ, admit you to the participation of the Lord's Supper, and to all the privileges of the new covenant.

The very God of peace sanctify you wholly; and I pray God your whole spirit, and soul, and body, be preserved blameless unto the coming of our Lord Jesus Christ.

Let us Pray.

ALMIGHTY God, who hast formed a Church in the world, and hast promised to perpetuate and protect it to the end of time, we thank Thee for Thy great mercy to these Thy children, and to Thy Church, to which Thou hast given the joy of receiving them into full communion. We thank Thee that from infancy, by Holy Baptism, they have been incorporated into the kingdom of Christ. We thank Thee for their Christian education, for the exhortation of parents and teachers, and that Thou hast spared them, and given them power this day to own and accept for themselves the covenant of salvation made with them before, in the sacrament of Baptism.

Forgive, O Lord, all the sins which they, in the foolishness of youth, have committed against Thee; and graciously accept them now dedicating themselves to Thee their Lord and God.

Strengthen them, we beseech Thee, through the Holy Spirit the Comforter, and daily increase in them the manifold gifts of Thy grace, the spirit of wisdom and understanding, the spirit of counsel and might, the spirit of knowledge and of the fear of the Lord. As they have vowed to be Thy servants, help them, Lord, to fulfil their vow, and to remain faithful to Thee. May they bring forth abundantly the fruits of the Spirit, so that Thy Church and people may be comforted and strengthened through them. Defend them from all heresy and schism, from apostasy and unbelief. When they approach Thy holy table, to partake of the most precious body and blood of Christ, may they receive a rich measure of Thy grace. And grant, O most merciful Father, that they may continue steadfast unto the end, and that their portion may be with Thy saints at the second and glorious appearing of our Lord and Saviour Jesus Christ.
Amen.

Then the Minister may add this Exhortation—

Dearly beloved,—Your eternal welfare depends upon the way in which you fulfil the engagements that you have now undertaken. I beseech you, therefore, to remember them throughout your whole life. Admitted to the privilege of full communion in the Church, walk worthy of your vocation. Fulfil your part as good soldiers of Christ, and strengthen your brethren, in whose ranks you now take your place. Remember that you are the temples of the Holy Ghost, and the members of Christ, and that you are bound to glorify Him with your bodies and spirits which He hath redeemed. Flee youthful lusts: give yourselves to piety, temperance, charity, and all the Christian graces. Obey those who are over you in the Lord; shun heresy and schism; and labour for the peace and prosperity of the Church.

That you may be enabled to be faithful, seek always the help of God; wait upon all His ordinances; live by His Word; and join watchfulness to prayer.

Thus devoting yourselves to your God and Saviour from your early years, you will find His yoke to be easy, and His burden light. God on His part will bless you. He will give you His peace which passeth all understanding. He will make all things work together for your good, and you will finally receive the crown of life.

Then the Minister shall bless them, saying thus—

The blessing of God Almighty, of the Father, the Son, and the Holy Ghost, be upon you, and remain with you for ever and ever.

Amen.

The Order

for the

Baptism of Adults.

The Minister begins the Service with the following sentence—

OUR help is in the name of the Lord, who made heaven and earth.

He then asks the person to be baptized—

Do you present yourself for Holy Baptism, desiring to be ingrafted into the body of Christ? *Ans.*—I do.

Then the Minister says—

Dearly beloved,—Attend to the words of the institution of this Holy Sacrament as delivered by our Lord and Saviour to His disciples, after His resurrection, and before His ascension to the right hand of God.

"All power is given unto me in heaven and in earth. Go ye, therefore, and teach all nations, baptizing them in the name of the Father, and of the Son, and of the Holy Ghost; teaching them to observe all things whatsoever I have commanded you: and, lo, I am with you alway, even unto the end of the world."

The Sacrament thus instituted is a sign and seal of our ingrafting into Christ, of remission of sin by His blood, and regeneration by His Spirit, of adoption, and resurrection unto everlasting life; and by it we are solemnly admitted, by Christ's appointment, into His Church, and enter into an engagement to be the Lord's.

Hence St Peter, on the day of Pentecost, called upon the people, saying, "Repent and be baptized, every one of you, in the name of Jesus Christ, for the remission of sins, and ye shall receive the gift of the Holy Ghost. For the promise is unto you, and to your children, and to all that are afar off, even as many as the Lord our God shall call."

He then says to the person to be baptized—

Forasmuch, then, as you are desirous of receiving this Holy Sacrament, it is necessary that you sincerely give answer, before God and His Church, to the questions I have now to ask.

Do you receive the doctrine of that holy faith into which you are now to be baptized, whereof we make confession, saying, "I believe in God the Father Almighty," &c.

These articles of the Christian faith, and the whole doctrine of the Old and New Testaments, you believe, and in this faith you desire to be baptized. Do you not?

Ans.—I do.

Do you, with heartfelt sorrow for your sins, renounce the devil, the world, and the flesh, and consecrate yourself to God as your Father, to Christ as your Saviour, and to the Holy Ghost as your Sanctifier, and promise to keep His commandments all the days of your life?

Ans.—I do.

Do you promise to submit yourself to all the ordinances of Christ, to use faithfully the means of grace, and to give to the relief of the poor, and the extension of the Church, as the Lord may prosper you?

Ans.—I do.

Or—

{ Do you therefore desire to be baptized in the name of the Father, and of the Son, and of the Holy Ghost; and do you promise to follow Christ, and keep His commandments all the days of your life?

Ans.—I do.

The Minister then says—

𝔏et us 𝔓ray.

ALMIGHTY and ever-living God, whose dearly-beloved Son, Jesus Christ our Lord, gave commandment to His apostles that they should go teach all nations, and baptize them in the name of the Father, and of the Son, and of the Holy Ghost; we humbly call upon Thee to bless Thine own ordinance now to be administered, and to ratify in heaven what by Thine appointment we do upon earth.

Look mercifully upon *this person*, we beseech Thee, that *he*, coming to Thy Holy Baptism, may receive remission of sin, and be born again of water and of the Holy Ghost. May *his* name be enrolled in the Lamb's book of life, never to be blotted out; and *he*, being planted into the likeness of the death and resurrection of Christ, may the body of sin be so destroyed in *him* that *he* may serve Thee in newness of life.

Sanctify this water to the spiritual use for which Thou hast ordained it; and grant, we beseech Thee, that *this person* now to be baptized therein may receive the fulness of Thy grace, and ever remain in the number of Thy faithful people; through Jesus Christ our Lord.
Amen.

Then the Minister asks the name of the Catechumen, and having caused him to kneel down, baptizes him, saying—

M. [or *N.*], I baptize thee in the name of the Father, and of the Son, and of the Holy Ghost.
Amen.

He then blesses the person baptized, thus—

The very God of peace sanctify you wholly: and I pray God your whole spirit, and soul, and body, be preserved blameless unto the coming of the Lord Jesus Christ.
Amen.

He then says—

This person is now received by Christ's appointment into His Church, to be a partaker of the Lord's Supper, and of all the privileges of the new covenant, and is engaged to confess the faith of Christ crucified, and to continue Christ's faithful soldier and servant unto *his* life's end.

Let us Pray.

WE yield Thee hearty thanks, most merciful Father, that it hath pleased Thee to deliver *this Thy servant* from the power of darkness, and to incorporate *him* into Thy holy Church, to be a partaker of the inestimable benefits purchased by the blood of Thy dear Son; and we beseech Thee to grant that being now ingrafted into Christ, the true vine, *he* may evermore abide in Him, and receive out of His fulness and grace for grace. Suffer *him* never to lose the force of *his* baptism, or to fall away from Thee, but may *he* fight the good fight of the faith, and constantly persevere in *his* holy profession.

Strengthen *him*, we beseech Thee, through the Holy Spirit the Comforter, and daily increase in *him* the manifold gifts of Thy grace, the spirit of wisdom and understanding, the spirit of counsel and might, the spirit of knowledge and of the fear of the Lord. As *he* has vowed to be Thy servant, help *him*, Lord, to fulfil *his* vow, and to remain faithful to Thee. May *he* bring forth abundantly the fruits of the Spirit, so that Thy Church and people may be comforted and strengthened through *him*. Defend *him* from all heresy and schism, from apostasy and unbelief. When *he* approaches Thy holy table, to partake of the most precious body and blood of Christ, may *he* receive a rich measure of Thy grace. And grant, O most merciful Father, that *he* may continue steadfast unto the end, and that *his* portion may be with Thy saints at the second and glorious appearing of our Lord and Saviour Jesus Christ.

Sanctify to all of us the administration of this Holy Sacrament. We look back with gratitude to our own Baptism, and bless Thee for the privileges and benefits conferred therein. We have to humble ourselves before Thee for our sinful defilement, our falling short of, and walking contrary to, the grace of Baptism and our solemn vows. But we beseech Thee to cleanse us from all our guilt by the blood of Christ, and to grant that henceforth, drawing strength from His death and resurrection for the mortifying of sin, and the quickening of grace, we may have our conversation in righteousness, and may walk in brotherly love, as being baptized by the same spirit into one body.

Our Father which art in heaven, Hallowed be Thy name. Thy kingdom come. Thy will be done in earth, as it is in heaven. Give us this day our daily bread. And forgive us our trespasses, as we forgive them that trespass against us. And lead us not into temptation; but deliver us from evil: For Thine is the kingdom, and the power, and the glory, for ever and ever.

Amen.

Then the Minister may add an Exhortation, as in p. 163.

The Order

of the

Celebration of the Lord's Supper

or

Holy Communion.

The Prayer after Sermon being ended, the Minister may give this Exhortation—

Dearly beloved,—As we are now about to celebrate the Holy Communion of the body and blood of Christ, let us consider how St Paul exhorteth all persons to examine themselves before they eat of that bread, and drink of that cup. For as the benefit is great, if with a truly penitent heart and lively faith we receive that holy sacrament (for then we spiritually eat the flesh of Christ, and drink His blood; then we dwell in Christ and Christ in us; we are one with

Christ and Christ with us), so is the danger great if we receive the same unworthily. For then we are guilty of the body and blood of Christ our Saviour; we eat and drink our own condemnation, not discerning the Lord's body.

Therefore, in the name of the eternal God, and of His Son Jesus Christ, whose minister I am, I warn all who are not of the number of the faithful, all who live in any sin against their knowledge or their conscience, charging them that they profane not this holy Table.

And yet this I pronounce, not to exclude any penitent person, how grievous soever his sins have been, but only such as continue in sin without repentance.

Examine your own consciences, therefore, to know whether you truly repent of your sins, and whether, trusting in God's mercy, and seeking your whole salvation in Jesus Christ, you are resolved to follow holiness, and to live in peace and charity with all men.

If you have this testimony in your hearts before God, I announce and declare that your sins are forgiven through the perfect merit of Jesus Christ our Lord; and I bid you, in His name, to His holy Table.

And although you feel that you have not perfect faith, and do not serve God with such zeal as you ought, but have daily to fight against the lusts of your flesh; yet if, by God's grace, you are heartily sorry for these weaknesses, and earnestly desire to withstand all unbelief, and to keep all His commandments, be assured that your remaining sins and infirmities do not prevent you from being received of God in mercy, and so made worthy partakers of this heavenly food.

For we come not to this Supper as righteous in ourselves, but we come to seek our life in Christ, acknowledging that we lie in the midst of death. Let us, then, look upon this Sacrament as a remedy for those who are sick, and consider that the worthiness our Lord requireth of us is, that we be truly sorry for our sins, and find our joy and salvation in Him. United with Him who is holy, even our Lord Jesus Christ, we are accepted of the Father, and invited to partake of these HOLY THINGS WHICH ARE FOR HOLY PERSONS.

Then the Minister gives out a hymn (35th Paraphrase).

The Holy Communion.

While the hymn is being sung, the Minister and Assistants bring in the elements and place them on the Communion Table [the alms are collected]; and the Communicants take their places at the Table.

Minister. — The grace of the Lord Jesus Christ, and the love of God, and the fellowship of the Holy Ghost, be with you all.

Amen.

Minister.—Beloved in the Lord, attend *The Institution.* to the words of the institution of the Holy Supper of our Lord Jesus Christ, as they are delivered by the holy apostle Paul (1 Cor. xi. 23-26): "I have received of the Lord that which also I delivered unto you, That the Lord Jesus the same night in which He was betrayed took bread: and when He had given thanks, He brake it, and said, Take, eat: this is my body, which is broken for you: this do in remembrance of me. After the same manner also He took the cup, when He had supped, saying, This cup is the new testament in my blood: this do ye, as oft as ye drink it, in remembrance of me. For as often as ye eat this bread, and drink this cup, ye do show the Lord's death till He come."

Dearly beloved,—You have heard in *The Address.* what manner the Lord hath instituted His Holy Supper, and how we are to remember Him by it.

Taking and setting apart these elements, by the Word and prayer, to be sacramentally the body and blood of Christ, we must be fully persuaded in our hearts of the mystery of His holy incarnation—God manifest in the flesh; that He was chosen by the Father to be Mediator, sent by Him into the world, and assumed our flesh and blood, as the second Adam, the Lord from heaven.

That having taken our nature, He endured for us the curse and punishment of sin, and thereby satisfied divine justice; that He was bound that we might be set free; was reviled that we might come to honour; was condemned that we might be acquitted at the judgment-seat of God; yea, that He suffered His blessed body to be nailed to the cross, and bowed His head in death, that we might be accepted of God and raised to life in Him;—and this one offering up of Himself once for all we are to commemorate and show forth in the breaking of bread, with a spiritual oblation of all possible praise unto God for the same.

And as the Lord hath ordained that we are to eat of this bread and drink of this cup, to assure us of our union with Him, and that He giveth us His body and His blood to be our meat and our drink unto life eternal, we are not to doubt His goodness, but to be firmly persuaded that He accomplisheth spiritually in us all that He outwardly exhibits. For "the cup of blessing which we bless, is it not the communion of the blood of Christ? the bread which we break, is it not the communion of the body of Christ?"

And as by His death, resurrection, and ascension, He hath obtained for us the life-giving Spirit, which, dwelling in Him as the Head, and in us as His members, unites us all in one body, we are to receive this Supper in brotherly love, and mindful of the communion of saints. "For we, being many, are one body; for we are all partakers of that one bread." We are to rejoice in the holy fellowship wherein we have part in the body of Christ, with the faithful patriarchs and prophets of old; the holy apostles and evangelists; the blessed martyrs and confessors; the redeemed of all ages who have died in the Lord, and now live with Him for evermore; our fathers, our brethren, our children, and the friends who were as our own souls: believing that though our eyes behold them no more, they have not perished, but that as "Jesus died and rose again, even so them also which sleep in Jesus will God bring with Him;" and that when the day breaks, and the shadows flee away, we shall meet them again in glory and in joy.

And now, that we may fulfil the Saviour's institution with righteousness and joy, let us, in celebrating this sacred service, follow His holy example in word and action.

As the Lord Jesus, the night in which He was betrayed, took bread, I take these elements to be set apart to the holy use and mystery for which He has appointed them,

[*Here the Minister may take the paten and the cup into his hand*]

and as He gave thanks and blessed, let us now draw near to the throne of grace, and present to God our

Prayers and Thanksgivings.

Profession of Faith. Almighty and eternal God, with Thy holy Church throughout all the world we believe in Thee the Father Almighty, Maker of heaven and earth; and in Jesus Christ Thine only Son our Lord, who was conceived by the Holy Ghost, born of the Virgin Mary, suffered under Pontius Pilate, was crucified, dead, and buried: He descended into hell; the third day He rose again from the dead; He ascended into heaven, and sitteth on the right hand of God the Father Almighty; from thence He shall come to judge the quick and the dead. We believe in the Holy Ghost; the holy Catholic Church; the communion of saints; the forgiveness of sins; the resurrection of the body; and the life everlasting.

Amen.

Lord, increase our faith.

Prayer of Access.

Almighty God, our heavenly Father, who admittest Thy people into such wonderful communion, that, partaking of the body and blood of Thy dear Son, they should dwell in Him, and He in them; we unworthy sinners, approaching Thy presence, and beholding Thy glory, do abhor ourselves, and repent in dust and ashes. We have grievously sinned against Thee in thought, in word, and in deed, provoking most justly Thy wrath and indignation against us. We have broken our past vows, we have dishonoured Thy holy name, and are unworthy of the least of all Thy mercies.

We confess, with the centurion, that we are not worthy that Thou shouldst come under our roof; and acknowledge, with that woman of Canaan, that we deserve not to eat of the crumbs which fall from Thy table.

Yet now, most gracious Father, have mercy upon us; for the sake of Jesus Christ forgive us all our sins; purify us from all uncleanness in spirit and in flesh; enable us heartily to forgive others as we beseech Thee to forgive us; and grant that we may hereafter serve Thee in newness of life to the glory of Thy holy name.

O God, who by the blood of Thy dear Son hast consecrated for us a new and living way into the holiest of all, grant unto us, we beseech Thee, the assurance of Thy mercy, and sanctify us by Thy Holy Spirit, that, drawing near unto

Thee in these holy mysteries with a pure heart and undefiled conscience, we may offer unto Thee a sacrifice in righteousness; through Jesus Christ our Lord.

Amen.

The Eucharistic Prayer. And now we lift up our hearts and minds on high, and give thanks unto Thee, the Lord our God. It is very meet, right, and our bounden duty, that we should at all times, and in all places, give thanks unto Thee, O eternal God, through Jesus Christ our Lord. For by Thy word Thou didst create heaven and earth, and all things therein: Thou didst also, at the first, make man after Thine own image and likeness; and by Thy providence we and all things living are sustained. For all Thy bounties known to us, for all unknown, we give Thee thanks; but chiefly that when, through disobedience, we had fallen from Thee, Thou didst not suffer us to depart from Thee for ever, but hast ransomed us from eternal death, and given us the joyful hope of everlasting life, through Jesus Christ Thy Son; who, being very and eternal God, dwelling with Thee before all time, in glory and blessedness unspeakable, came down from heaven in perfect love, and became man for us men, and for our salvation.

Not as we ought, but as we are able, we bless Thee for His holy incarnation; for His life on earth; for His precious sufferings and death upon the cross; for His resurrection from the dead; and for His glorious ascension to Thy right hand.

We bless Thee for the giving of the Holy Ghost; for the sacraments and ordinances of the Church; for the communion of Christ's body and blood; for the great hope of everlasting life, and of an eternal weight of glory.

Thee, mighty God, heavenly King, we magnify and praise. With angels and archangels, and all the hosts of heaven, we worship and adore Thy glorious name, joining in the everlasting hymn of the cherubim and seraphim, and singing unto Thee:

Holy, holy, holy, Lord God of Sabaoth; heaven and earth are full of Thy glory. Hosanna in the highest. Blessed is He that cometh in the name of the Lord. Hosanna in the highest.

The Invocation. And we most humbly beseech Thee, O merciful Father, to vouchsafe unto us Thy gracious presence, as we now make that memorial of His most blessed sacrifice which Thy Son hath commanded us to make: and to bless and sanctify with Thy Word and Spirit these Thine own gifts of bread and wine which we set before Thee; that we, receiving them, according to our Saviour's institution, in thankful remembrance of His death and passion, may, through the power of the Holy Ghost, be very partakers of His body and blood, with all His benefits, to our salvation and the glory of Thy most holy name.

Amen.

The Lord's Prayer. Our Father which art in heaven, Hallowed be Thy name. Thy kingdom come. Thy will be done in earth, as it is in heaven. Give us this day our daily bread. And forgive us our trespasses, as we forgive them that trespass against us. And lead us not into temptation; but deliver us from evil: For Thine is the kingdom, and the power, and the glory, for ever and ever.

Amen.

Minister.—According to the holy institution, example, and command of OUR LORD JESUS CHRIST, and in remembrance of Him, we do this—WHO, THE SAME NIGHT IN WHICH HE WAS BETRAYED, TOOK BREAD:

Here he shall take some of the bread into his hands—

AND WHEN HE HAD GIVEN THANKS, HE BRAKE IT,

Here he shall break the bread—

AND SAID, TAKE, EAT: THIS IS MY BODY WHICH IS BROKEN FOR YOU: THIS DO IN REMEMBRANCE OF ME.

Here he shall himself partake, and shall distribute the bread to the assistants. Then he shall say—

AFTER THE SAME MANNER ALSO HE TOOK THE CUP,

Here he shall take the cup into his hand—

WHEN HE HAD SUPPED, SAYING, THIS CUP IS THE NEW TESTAMENT IN MY BLOOD: THIS DO YE, AS OFT AS YE DRINK IT, IN REMEMBRANCE OF ME.

Here the cup is to be given. When one and all have received, the Minister shall say—

The peace of the Lord Jesus Christ be with you all.

If there be more than can be accommodated at one time, the first company of communicants then withdraw, singing the ciii. Psalm, and others take their places—and the service is renewed as before, till all have communicated. With all companies after the first, the Minister shall begin at the words, "Take, eat," &c.

THE HOLY COMMUNION.

Exhortation to Thankfulness. Beloved in the Lord, since the Lord hath now fed our souls at His Table, let us praise His holy name with thanksgiving, who hath not spared His own Son, but delivered Him for us all, and given us all things with Him: who commendeth His love toward us, in that, while we were yet sinners, Christ died for us; much more then, being now justified by His blood, we shall be saved from wrath through Him. For if, when we were enemies, we were reconciled to God by the death of His Son; much more, being reconciled, we shall be saved by His life. Let us therefore show forth His praise from this time forth for evermore, glorifying God in our bodies and in our spirits, which are His; ever walking worthy of His grace, and of our high calling in Christ Jesus.

Let us Pray.

Prayer of Thanks and Self-Dedication. ALMIGHTY and everlasting God, we most heartily thank Thee that Thou hast now vouchsafed to feed us with the spiritual food of the most precious body and blood of Thy Son our Saviour Jesus Christ, assuring us thereby that we are very members incorporate in the mystical body of Thy Son, and heirs through hope of Thine everlasting kingdom. And we beseech Thee, O heavenly Father, so to assist us with Thy grace that we may continue in that holy fellowship, and do all such good works as Thou hast before ordained that we should walk in them; through Jesus Christ our Lord.

We offer and present ourselves unto Thee, our souls and our bodies, and dedicate ourselves wholly to Thy service, henceforth to live only to Thy glory. Thou art our God, and we will praise Thee: Thou art our God, we will exalt Thee.

Intercession for the Church militant. O God, the Father of our Lord Jesus Christ, of whom the whole family in heaven and in earth is named, we desire at this time, gathered around Thy holy Table, to remember before Thee all with whom we have part in the communion of Thy saints; and we beseech Thee, in consideration of the sacrifice which we have now commemorated, that Thou wouldst receive the supplications which we offer unto Thy divine majesty.

Look down in mercy, we beseech Thee, on Thy Church militant here upon earth.

Give grace, O heavenly Father, unto all who bear office in Thy Church, that they may fulfil their several ministries in Thy fear, and in purity of heart; and to all Thy people, that they may be holy and obedient, and may come behind in no gift, waiting for the coming of our Lord Jesus Christ.

[Especially we commend unto Thee the pastor of this parish, and the people therein, beseeching Thee to accept and increase their piety and faith.]

O merciful God, look down upon Thy desolate heritage, upon Thy scattered and divided people. Put away all schisms and heresies from among them; cleanse Thy sanctuary from all defilement of superstition, will-worship, and infidelity, and grant unto all that seek Thee the joy and comfort of the Holy Ghost, and unto Thy whole Church unity and peace.

We pray for all estates of men in Christian lands; for kings, princes, and governors; for nobles and men of estate, and for all the people; and we beseech Thee so to dispose the affairs of all nations that righteousness and truth may prevail, and that we may lead quiet and peaceable lives in all godliness and honesty. Especially we pray for our country; for Thy servant her most sacred Majesty Queen Victoria, for Albert Edward Prince of Wales, the Princess of Wales, and all the Royal Family.

Send forth the news of Thy salvation unto the ends of the earth, and turn the hearts of men everywhere, that they may become obedient to the faith.

Vouchsafe unto us seasonable weather; give

and preserve to our use the fruits of the earth; and save us from war, pestilence, and famine.

Comfort and succour, we beseech Thee, all Thy people who are in trouble, sorrow, need, sickness, or any other adversity.

And especially we commend unto Thee those departing this life: be present to them, in Thy mercy and Thy love, in that last hour when heart and flesh do fail; defend them against the assaults of the devil, and give them such patient hope and confidence that they may joyfully commit their spirits to Thy hands, and do Thou receive them to Thy rest.

Thanks for the Church triumphant. And rejoicing in the communion of Thy saints, we bless Thy holy name for all Thy servants who have departed in the faith, and who, having accomplished their warfare, are at rest with Thee. We yield unto Thee most high praise and hearty thanks for Thy great grace and many gifts bestowed on them who have been the lights of the world in their several generations, beseeching Thee to enable us so to follow their faith and good example, that we with them may finally be partakers of Thy heavenly kingdom; when, made like unto Christ, we shall behold Him with unveiled face, rejoicing in His glory; and by Him we, with all Thy Church, holy and unspotted, shall be presented with exceeding

joy before the presence of Thy glory. Hear us, O heavenly Father, for His sake: to whom, with Thee and the Holy Ghost, be glory for ever and ever.
Amen.

Then may be sung the Song of Simeon.

The Benediction. Now the God of peace, that brought again from the dead our Lord Jesus, that great Shepherd of the sheep, through the blood of the everlasting covenant, make you perfect in every good work to do His will, working in you that which is well-pleasing in His sight, through Jesus Christ; to whom be glory for ever and ever.
Amen.

The Order

of the

Solemnization of Matrimony.

The persons to be married being present "in the place appointed for public worship," with a sufficient number of witnesses, the man standing on the right hand and the woman on the left,

The Minister shall say—

OUR help is in the name of the Lord, who made heaven and earth.

Dearly beloved,—We are here gathered together in the sight of God, and in the face of this congregation, to join together this man and this woman in the bonds of matrimony, which is a holy estate instituted by God in the time of man's innocency; which was beautified and adorned by our Lord's gracious presence and first miracle at the wedding in Cana of Galilee; which is commended by St Paul as honourable in all, and consecrated as signifying unto us the mystical union that subsists between Christ and His Church.

It is therefore not to be entered on lightly, nor unadvisedly, but thoughtfully, reverently, and in the fear of God, with due consideration of the reasons for which it was ordained, and the duties which it imposes.

These you find plainly set forth in God's holy Word, wherein it is said :—

"Wives, submit yourselves unto your own husbands, as unto the Lord. For the husband is the head of the wife, even as Christ is the Head of the Church: and He is the saviour of the body. Therefore as the Church is subject unto Christ, so let the wives be to their own husbands in everything. Husbands, love your wives, even as Christ also loved the Church, and gave Himself for it; that He might sanctify and cleanse it with the washing of water by the Word, that He might present it to Himself a glorious Church, not having spot, or wrinkle, or any such thing; but that it should be holy and without blemish. So ought men to love their wives as their own bodies. He that loveth his wife loveth himself. For no man ever yet hated his own flesh; but nourisheth and cherisheth it, even as the Lord the Church:

for we are members of His body, of His flesh, and of His bones. For this cause shall a man leave his father and mother, and shall be joined unto his wife, and they two shall be one flesh. This is a great mystery: but I speak concerning Christ and the Church. Nevertheless let every one of you in particular so love his wife even as himself; and the wife see that she reverence her husband."

Into this holy estate these two persons are now come to be joined.

Therefore if any man can show any just cause why they may not lawfully be joined together, let him now declare the same.

Then speaking to the persons that are to be married, he shall say—

Also I require and charge you both, as ye will answer at the day of judgment, when the secrets of all hearts shall be disclosed, that if either of you know any impediment why ye may not be lawfully joined together in matrimony, ye do now confess it. For be ye well assured that so many as are coupled together otherwise than God's Word doth allow, are not joined together by God; neither is their marriage lawful.

If no impediment be alleged or confessed, the Minister shall say—

Let us Pray.

ALMIGHTY and most merciful Father, we Thy sinful and unworthy children praise Thee for all the gifts of Thy providence, and for all the bounties of Thy grace. Especially do we at this time thank Thee for the institution of marriage, and that Thou hast made it to be honourable in all. And we humbly beseech Thee graciously to send down Thy blessing upon these Thy servants who are about to be joined together according to Thy holy institution and ordinance. As Thou hast brought them together by Thy providence, sanctify them by Thy Spirit, giving them a new frame of heart, fit for their new estate, and enriching them with all grace, whereby they may perform the duties, enjoy the comforts, undergo the cares, and resist the temptations, which accompany that condition, as becometh Christians. May they enter into the marriage covenant in Thy fear, and truly keep the vows which they are about to make, according to Thy Word. Grant this, O our Father, with the forgiveness of all our sins, through Jesus Christ our Lord.

Amen.

Then the Minister shall say—

As a seal to the holy vow which you are about to make, give each other the right hand; and say after me—

He shall then cause the man, holding the woman by the right hand, to repeat these words—

I, A., do take thee, C., to be my married wife; and do, in the presence of God, and before this congregation, promise and covenant to be a loving and faithful husband unto thee, until God shall separate us by death.

Then the woman, holding the man by the right hand, shall say—

I, C., do take thee, A., to be my married husband; and do, in the presence of God, and before this congregation, promise and covenant to be a loving, faithful, and obedient wife unto thee, until God shall separate us by death.

[The Minister may then add—

In token of fidelity to these vows, this ring is given and received.

Then the man shall place the ring on the fourth finger of the woman's left hand.]

Then the Minister shall say—

Forasmuch as you have covenanted together in holy wedlock, and have declared the same before God and these witnesses, I pronounce you to be husband and wife: In the name of the Father, and of the Son, and of the Holy Ghost.

Amen.

Those whom God hath joined together, let not man put asunder.

Then shall he bless them.

Almighty God, who at the beginning did create our first parents, Adam and Eve, and did sanctify and join them in marriage, pour down upon you the riches of His grace, sanctify and bless you that you may please Him both in body and soul, and live together in holy love, unto your lives' end.

Amen.

Then the Minister may add an exhortation, or short sermon, and thereafter shall say—

Let us Pray.

O GOD, the author and giver of all good things, who hast consecrated this estate of marriage, and made it holy, by Thine own institution and blessing, and by the mystery whereby it sets forth the union of all faithful souls with Jesus Christ, our great Husband and Head; let Thy blessing, we humbly entreat Thee, descend and rest upon these Thy servants, who have now been joined together. Grant unto them health, peace, and prosperity. May they dwell together in unity and love all the days of their life. [Give them a lasting posterity, and bless them in their children.] Give them of the dew of heaven above and of the fatness of the earth below; fill their dwelling with corn and wine and oil, and all good things, that they may give to the needy of what they possess. And, above all things, O Lord, we pray Thee to enrich their souls with Thy heavenly grace, that they may obey and serve Thee all their days, walking in the steps of Jesus Christ Thy Son, and adorning His doctrine; that, finally, when the joys and sorrows, and all the good and evil, of this transitory world are ended, they may inherit Thy promises, and be made partakers of eternal joy in Thy glorious kingdom, where they neither marry nor are given in marriage, but are as the angels of God in heaven.

O Lord Almighty, who dost invite us all, in Thy Gospel, to the great marriage-supper of Thy Son, so incline our hearts by Thy good Spirit, that we may yield obedience to Thy gracious call and come to the wedding; and may we, each one, be so clothed in the garments of righteousness and true holiness, that we may be accepted of Thee, and may sit down with Abraham, and Isaac, and Jacob, and all Thy saints, to enjoy for ever that banquet of unutterable felicity, which Thou hast prepared for them that love Thee.

O Thou, whose only Son, Jesus Christ our Lord, did first display His divine power by turning water into wine at that marriage in Cana of Galilee which He beautified with His presence, turn, we pray Thee, the water into wine, to us Thy servants; that all our temporal mercies, being sanctified to us, may become spiritual blessings, and means of life and salvation; through Jesus Christ our Redeemer.

Amen.

Our Father which art in heaven, Hallowed be Thy name. Thy kingdom come. Thy will be done in earth, as it is in heaven. Give us this day our daily bread. And forgive us our trespasses, as we forgive them that trespass against us. And lead us not into temptation; but deliver us from evil: For Thine is the kingdom, and the power, and the glory, for ever and ever.

Amen.

[*Here the lxvii. or the cxxviii. Psalm may be said, or sung.*]

The peace of God, which passeth all understanding, keep your hearts and minds in the knowledge and love of God and of His Son Jesus Christ our Lord; and the blessing of God Almighty, the Father, the Son, and the Holy Ghost, be amongst you and remain with you always.

Amen.

The Order of Divine Service

at the

Burial of the Dead.

The Minister may begin the service at the house, or church, with one or more of these sentences—

OUR help is in the name of the Lord, who made heaven and earth.

It is better to go to the house of mourning than to go to the house of feasting; for that is the end of all men, and the living will lay it to his heart.

Naked came I out of my mother's womb, and naked shall I return thither: the Lord gave, and the Lord hath taken away; blessed be the name of the Lord.

All flesh is grass, and all the glory of man as the flower of grass. The grass withereth, and the flower thereof falleth away; but the word of the Lord endureth for ever.

I am the Resurrection and the Life: saith the Lord. He that believeth in me, though he were dead, yet shall he live; and whosoever liveth and believeth in me shall never die.

He may then read one or more of the collections of Scripture which follow, saying—

Let us hear the Word of God, written for our admonition and comfort.

I.

What man is he that liveth, and shall not see death? Shall he deliver his soul from the hand of the grave? One dieth in his full strength, being wholly at ease and quiet; another dieth in the bitterness of his soul, and never eateth with pleasure: they shall lie down alike in the dust, and the worms shall cover them. All flesh shall perish together, and man shall turn again into dust.—Ps. lxxxix. 48; Job, xxi. 23, 25, 26, xxxii. 15.

There is hope of a tree, if it be cut down, that it will sprout again, and that the tender branch thereof will not cease. Though the root thereof wax old in the earth, and the stock thereof die in the ground; yet through the scent of water it will bring forth boughs like a plant. But man dieth, and wasteth away; yea, man giveth up the ghost, and where is he? As the waters fail from the sea, and the flood decayeth and drieth up: so man lieth down, and riseth not: till the heavens be no more they shall not awake, nor be raised out of their sleep.—Job, xiv. 7-12.

The righteous hath hope in his death. Let me die the death of the righteous, and let my last end be like his. Precious in the sight of the Lord is the death of His saints. They shall hunger no more, neither thirst any more; neither shall the sun light on them, nor any heat. And there shall be no more death, neither sorrow nor crying, neither shall there be any more pain: for the former things are passed away. And God shall wipe away all tears from their eyes. —Prov. xiv. 32; Num. xxiii. 10; Ps. cxvi. 15; Rev. vii. 16, xxi. 4, vii. 17.

II.

Man is like to vanity: his days are as a shadow that passeth away. His breath goeth forth, he returneth to his earth; in that very day his thoughts perish.—Ps. cxliv. 4, cxlvi. 4.

When he dieth he shall carry nothing away; his glory shall not descend after him. As he came forth from his mother's womb, naked shall he return to go as he came, and he shall take nothing of his labour which he may carry away in his hand. We brought nothing into this world, and it is certain we can carry nothing out.—Ps. xlix. 17; Eccles. v. 15; 1 Tim. vi. 7.

What is your life? It is even a vapour which appeareth for a little time, and then vanisheth away. Our days on earth are as a shadow, and there is none abiding. We all do fade as a leaf, and our iniquities like the wind have taken us away.—James, iv. 14; 1 Chron. xxix. 15; Isa. lxiv. 6.

Brethren, the time is short; it remaineth that they that weep be as though they wept not; and they that rejoice, as though they rejoiced not; and they that buy, as though they possessed not; and they that use this world as not abusing it: for the fashion of this world passeth away.—1 Cor. vii. 29-31.

The night cometh when no man can work. Whatsoever thy hand findeth to do, do it with thy might; for there is no work, nor device, nor wisdom, nor knowledge, in the grave, whither thou goest. Seek ye the Lord while He may be found, call ye upon Him while He is near: let the wicked forsake his way, and the unrighteous man his thoughts; and let him return unto the Lord, and He will have mercy upon him; and to our God, for He will abundantly pardon. The wages of sin is death; but the gift of God is eternal life through Jesus Christ our Lord. —John, ix. 4; Eccles. ix. 10; Isa. lv. 6, 7; Rom. vi. 23.

III.

Shall we receive good at the hand of the Lord, and shall we not receive evil? Behold, happy is the man whom God correcteth; therefore despise not thou the chastening of the Almighty; for He maketh sore, and bindeth up; He woundeth, and His hands make whole.— Job, ii. 10, v. 17, 18.

Will the Lord cast off for ever? and will He be favourable no more? Is His mercy clean gone for ever? doth His promise fail for evermore? Hath God forgotten to be gracious? hath He in anger shut up His tender mercies? —Ps. lxxvii. 7-9.

The Lord will not cast off for ever. For His merciful kindness is great toward us, and the truth of the Lord endureth for ever. The Lord is merciful and gracious, slow to anger, and plenteous in mercy. He will not always chide; neither will He keep His anger for ever. He hath not dealt with us after our sins; nor rewarded us according to our iniquities: for as the heaven is high above the earth, so great is His mercy toward them that fear Him. As far as the east is from the west, so far hath He removed our transgressions from us. Like as a father pitieth his children, so the Lord pitieth them that fear Him; for He knoweth our frame, He remembereth that we are dust. The mercy of the Lord is from everlasting to everlasting upon them that fear Him, and His righteousness unto children's children; to such as keep His covenant, and to those that remember His commandments to do them. A father of the fatherless, and a judge of the widows, is God in His holy habitation. Leave thy fatherless children, saith the Lord, I will preserve them alive; and let thy widows trust in me.—Lam. iii. 31; Ps. ciii. 8-18, lxviii. 5; Jer. xlix. 11.

When thou art in tribulation, if thou turn to the Lord thy God, and shalt be obedient unto His voice, the Lord thy God is a merciful God; He will not forsake thee, nor destroy thee. And thou shalt remember all the way which the Lord thy God led thee, to humble thee, and to prove thee, to know what was in thine heart, whether thou wouldest keep His commandments or no. Thou shalt also consider, that as a man chasteneth his son, so the Lord thy God chasteneth thee. That the trial of your faith being much more precious than of gold that perisheth, though it be tried with fire, might be found unto praise, and honour, and glory, at the appearing of Jesus Christ.—Deut. iv. 30, 31, viii. 2, 5; 1 Peter, i. 7.

IV.

Now is Christ risen from the dead, and become the first-fruits of them that slept. For since by man came death, by man came also the resurrection of the dead. For as in Adam all die, even so in Christ shall all be made alive. But every man in his own order: Christ the first-fruits; afterward they that are Christ's at His coming.

Then cometh the end, when He shall have delivered up the kingdom to God, even the Father; when He shall have put down all rule, and all authority and power. For He must reign till He hath put all enemies under His feet. The last enemy that shall be destroyed is death. For He hath put all things under His feet. But when He saith, All things are put under Him, it is manifest that He is excepted which did put all things under Him. And when all things shall be subdued unto Him, then shall the Son also Himself be subject unto Him that put all things under Him, that God may be all in all.

But some man will say, How are the dead raised up? and with what body do they come?

Thou fool, that which thou sowest is not quickened except it die. And that which thou sowest, thou sowest not that body that shall be, but bare grain, it may chance of wheat, or of some other grain; but God giveth it a body as it hath pleased Him, and to every seed his own body. All flesh is not the same flesh: but there is one kind of flesh of men, another flesh of beasts, another of fishes, and another of birds. There are also celestial bodies, and bodies terrestrial: but the glory of the celestial is one, and the glory of the terrestrial is another. There is one glory of the sun, and another glory of the moon, and another glory of the stars; for one star differeth from another star in glory. So also is the resurrection of the dead: it is sown in corruption, it is raised in incorruption: it is sown in dishonour, it is raised in glory: it is sown in weakness, it is raised in power: it is sown a natural body, it is raised a spiritual body. There is a natural body, and there is a spiritual body. And so it is written, The first Adam was made a living soul; the last Adam was made a quickening spirit. Howbeit that was not first which is spiritual, but that which is natural; and afterward that which is spiritual. The first man is of the earth, earthy; the second man is the Lord from heaven. As is the earthy, such are they also that are earthy: and as is the heavenly, such are they also that are heavenly.

And as we have borne the image of the earthy, we shall also bear the image of the heavenly. Now this I say, brethren, that flesh and blood cannot inherit the kingdom of God; neither doth corruption inherit incorruption. Behold, I show you a mystery; We shall not all sleep, but we shall all be changed, in a moment, in the twinkling of an eye, at the last trump (for the trumpet shall sound); and the dead shall be raised incorruptible, and we shall be changed. For this corruptible must put on incorruption, and this mortal must put on immortality. So when this corruptible shall have put on incorruption, and this mortal shall have put on immortality, then shall be brought to pass the saying that is written, Death is swallowed up in victory. O death, where is thy sting? O grave, where is thy victory? The sting of death is sin; and the strength of sin is the law. But thanks be to God, which giveth us the victory through our Lord Jesus Christ. Therefore, my beloved brethren, be ye steadfast, unmovable, always abounding in the work of the Lord, forasmuch as ye know that your labour is not in vain in the Lord.—1 Cor. xv.

V.

Our light affliction, which is but for a moment, worketh for us a far more exceeding and eternal weight of glory; while we look not at the things which are seen, but at the things which are not seen: for the things which are seen are temporal, but the things which are not seen are eternal. For we know that if our earthly house of this tabernacle were dissolved, we have a building of God, an house not made with hands, eternal in the heavens. For in this we groan, earnestly desiring to be clothed upon with our house which is from heaven: if so be that being clothed we shall not be found naked. For we that are in this tabernacle do groan, being burdened; not for that we would be unclothed, but clothed upon, that mortality might be swallowed up of life. Now He that hath wrought us for the self-same thing is God, who also hath given unto us the earnest of the Spirit. Therefore we are always confident, knowing that, whilst we are at home in the body, we are absent from the Lord (for we walk by faith, not by sight): we are confident, I say, and willing rather to be absent from the body, and to be present with the Lord. Wherefore we labour, that whether present or absent, we may be accepted of Him. For we must all appear before the judgment-seat of Christ; that every one may receive the things done in his body, according to that he hath done, whether it be good or bad.—2 Cor. iv. 17, 18; v. 1-10.

I would not have you to be ignorant, brethren, concerning them which are asleep, that ye sorrow not, even as others which have no hope. For if we believe that Jesus died and rose again, even so them also which sleep in Jesus will God bring with Him. For this we say unto you by the word of the Lord, that we which are alive and remain unto the coming of the Lord, shall not prevent them which are asleep. For the Lord Himself shall descend from heaven with a shout, with the voice of the archangel, and with the trump of God; and the dead in Christ shall rise first: then we which are alive and remain shall be caught up together with them in the clouds, to meet the Lord in the air: and so shall we ever be with the Lord. Wherefore comfort one another with these words.—1 Thess. iv. 13-18.

VI.

AT THE BURIAL OF A CHILD.

And the Lord struck the child that Uriah's wife bare unto David, and it was very sick. David therefore besought God for the child;

and David fasted, and went in, and lay all night upon the earth. And the elders of his house arose, and went to him to raise him up from the earth: but he would not, neither did he eat bread with them. And it came to pass on the seventh day, that the child died. And the servants of David feared to tell him that the child was dead: for they said, Behold, while the child was yet alive, we spake unto him, and he would not hearken unto our voice: how will he then vex himself, if we tell him that the child is dead? But when David saw that his servants whispered, David perceived that the child was dead: therefore David said unto his servants, Is the child dead? And they said, He is dead. Then David arose from the earth, and washed, and anointed himself, and changed his apparel, and came into the house of the Lord, and worshipped: then he came to his own house; and when he required, they set bread before him, and he did eat. Then said his servants unto him, What thing is this that thou hast done? Thou didst fast and weep for the child, while it was alive; but when the child was dead, thou didst rise and eat bread. And he said, While the child was yet alive, I fasted and wept: for I said, Who can tell whether God will be gracious to me, that the child may live? But now he is dead, wherefore should I fast? can I bring him back again? I shall go to him, but he shall not return to me. —2 Sam. xii. 15-23.

Jesus said, Suffer little children, and forbid them not, to come unto me: for of such is the kingdom of heaven. It is not the will of your Father which is in heaven that one of these little ones should perish. For I say unto you, That in heaven their angels do always behold the face of my Father which is in heaven.—Matt. xix. 14; xviii. 14, 10.

O Lord, our Lord, how excellent is Thy name in all the earth! Out of the mouth of babes and sucklings Thou hast perfected praise. I thank Thee, O Father, Lord of heaven and earth, because Thou hast hid these things from the wise and prudent, and hast revealed them unto babes: even so, Father, for so it seemed good in Thy sight.—Ps. viii. 1, 2; Luke x. 21.

We have not an High Priest which cannot be touched with the feeling of our infirmities; but was in all points tempted like as we are, yet without sin. Let us therefore come boldly unto the throne of grace, that we may obtain mercy, and find grace to help in time of need.—Heb. iv. 15, 16.

The Lord gave, and the Lord hath taken away: blessed be the name of the Lord.—Job, i. 21.

Then may follow one or more of these Prayers.

ETERNAL and ever-blessed God, supreme Disposer of events, out of the depths of our sin and sorrow, we, the frail children of the dust, would lift up our souls unto Thee.

Through all time and change Thou art the same; irresistible in might, yet infinite in wisdom, love, and mercy; our refuge and our strength; our hope, and help, and comfort; our God and Father in Christ.

Clouds and darkness are round about Thee, but justice and judgment are the habitation of Thy throne: mercy and truth go before Thy face. Though Thou slay us, yet will we trust in Thee. Our flesh and our heart fail; but Thou art the strength of our heart, and our portion for ever.

Blessed be Thy name, O God, that in Thine unspeakable love Thou didst send Thy well-beloved Son into this world to be our Saviour, that even as sin had reigned unto death, so grace might reign through righteousness unto eternal life, by Jesus Christ our Lord.

Father of mercies and God of all comfort, who dost not afflict willingly the children of men, but lovest those whom Thou chastenest, draw near, we earnestly beseech Thee, with Thine own abundant consolations, to those who are sorrowing for the dead, so that while they mourn, they may not murmur, or faint under Thy rod; but, remembering Thine unnumbered past and present mercies, Thy promises, and all Thy love in Christ, may resign themselves meekly into Thy hands, to be taught and disciplined by Thee. Thou, Lord, knowest their condition, their sorrows, and the secrets of their hearts. Pour into their wounded spirits the balm of Thy fatherly wisdom and compassion; and grant that, loosened from earthly ties, they may cleave the more closely to Thee, who bringest life out of death, and who canst turn their grief into eternal joy.

Here may be introduced such special prayers or petitions as are proper to the occasion.

And now, O merciful God, vouchsafe unto us, who are still spared, grace to receive aright the warnings of Thy providence, and the lessons taught us by the life and death of our fellow-men. May every instance of mortality convince us of the evil of sin, and the vanity of earthly things, and lead us unto Him in whom pardon, peace, and life are to be found, so that we may be delivered from both the power of sin and the fear of death. And grant that, whensoever our call shall come, our souls may depart in peace, and our bodies rest in hope to rise in glory, through the might and merits of Jesus Christ our Saviour; for whom, and through whom, we desire, in life and in death, to bless Thy name;

and to whom, with Thee and the Holy Ghost, we would ascribe all glory and praise, world without end.

Amen.

O MERCIFUL God, Father of our Lord Jesus Christ, who hath said, Blessed are they that mourn, for they shall be comforted: under the shadow of Thy judgments we come to Thee, and acknowledge Thee to be the Lord alone. Thou hast entered this house with Thy chastenings. O be Thou nigh in Thy tender compassion to these afflicted ones. Bless Thy sorrowing servants with Thine abounding consolations. Convert them wholly to Thyself, and fill their bleeding hearts with Thy love. Make the night of their grief to be light by Thy grace. Deliver us, Thy servants, we pray Thee, from the bondage of our sins, that we may be free from fear of death, and may be ready at Thy coming. Yea, Lord, for Christ's sake, sanctify us by Thy Holy Spirit, that whether we live, we may live unto the Lord, or whether we die, we may die unto the Lord; whether we live or die, may we be the Lord's.

Amen.

O GOD, whose days are without end, and whose mercies cannot be numbered, make us, we beseech Thee, deeply sensible of the

shortness and uncertainty of human life, and let Thy Holy Spirit lead us through this vale of misery in holiness and righteousness all the days of our lives; that when we shall have served Thee in our generation, we may be gathered unto our fathers, having the testimony of a good conscience; in the communion of the Catholic Church; in the confidence of a certain faith; in the comfort of a reasonable, religious, and holy hope, in favour with Thee our God, and in perfect charity with the world: all which we ask through Jesus Christ our Lord.
Amen.

Our Father which art in heaven, Hallowed be Thy name. Thy kingdom come. Thy will be done in earth, as it is in heaven. Give us this day our daily bread. And forgive us our trespasses, as we forgive them that trespass against us. And lead us not into temptation; but deliver us from evil: For Thine is the kingdom, and the power, and the glory, for ever and ever.
Amen.

After the Prayer, if it be convenient, there may be sung, or chanted, the 39th, 90th, or 139th Psalm, or the 53d Paraphrase, or the 156th or 157th Hymn. If the service is to be concluded in the house, or church, the Minister may then say (as on page 217), "Forasmuch, . . . we therefore go forth to commit," &c., until "they rest from their labours," on page 218, and shall then add—

Now the God of peace, that brought again from the dead our Lord Jesus Christ, that great Shepherd of the sheep, through the blood of the everlasting covenant, make you perfect in every good work to do His will, working in you that which is well-pleasing in His sight, through Jesus Christ; to whom be glory for ever and ever.

Amen.

[*If it be convenient, the following Service may be used at the grave.*]

When the body has been brought to the grave, the Minister may say—

MAN that is born of a woman hath but a short time to live, and is full of misery. He cometh up, and is cut down like a flower; he fleeth as it were a shadow, and never continueth in one stay.

In the midst of life we are in death: of whom may we seek for succour, but of Thee, O Lord, who for our sins are justly displeased?

Yet, O Lord God most holy, O Lord most

mighty, O holy and most merciful Saviour, deliver us not into the bitter pains of eternal death.

Thou knowest, Lord, the secrets of our hearts; shut not Thy merciful ears to our prayer, but spare us, Lord most holy, O God most mighty; O holy and merciful Saviour, Thou most worthy Judge eternal, suffer us not at our last hour, for any pains of death, to fall from Thee.

When the body has been laid in the grave he shall say—

Forasmuch as it hath pleased Almighty God, in His wise providence, to take out of this world the soul of our deceased *brother*, we therefore commit *his* body to the ground; earth to earth, ashes to ashes, dust to dust; looking for the general resurrection in the last day, and the life of the world to come, through our Lord Jesus Christ; at whose second coming in glorious majesty, to judge the world, the earth and sea shall give up their dead; and the corruptible bodies of those who sleep in Him shall be changed, and made like unto His own glorious body, according to the mighty working whereby He is able to subdue all things unto Himself.*

---

* *At the burial of the dead at sea, instead of the words*, We therefore commit *his* body to the ground, earth to earth, &c., *shall be said*, We therefore commit *his* body to the deep, to be turned into corruption, looking for the general resurrection, &c.

I heard a voice from heaven saying unto me, Write, From henceforth blessed are the dead which die in the Lord; even so, saith the Spirit, for they rest from their labours.

Blessed be the God and Father of our Lord, Jesus Christ, which according to His abundant mercy hath begotten us again unto a lively hope by the resurrection of Jesus Christ from the dead, to an inheritance incorruptible, and undefiled, and that fadeth not away.

Let us Pray.

ALMIGHTY God, with whom do live the spirits of them that depart hence in the Lord, and with whom the souls of the faithful, after they are delivered from the burden of the flesh, are in joy and felicity; we give Thee hearty thanks that it pleaseth Thee to deliver them out of the miseries of this sinful world; beseeching Thee, of Thy gracious goodness, shortly to accomplish the number of Thine elect, and to hasten Thy kingdom; that we, with all those that are departed in the true faith of Thy holy name, may have our perfect consummation and bliss, both in body and soul, in Thine eternal and everlasting glory; through Jesus Christ our Lord.

Amen.

O merciful God, the Father of our Lord Jesus Christ, who is the Resurrection and the Life; in whom whosoever believeth shall live, though he die; and whosoever liveth and believeth in Him shall not die eternally; who also hath taught us by His holy apostle St Paul, not to be sorry, as men without hope, for them that sleep in Him; we meekly beseech Thee, O Father, to raise us from the death of sin unto the life of righteousness; that, when we shall depart this life, we may rest in Him; and that, at the general resurrection in the last day, we may be found acceptable in Thy sight, and receive that blessing which Thy well-beloved Son shall then pronounce to all that love and fear Thee, saying, Come, ye blessed children of my Father, receive the kingdom prepared for you from the beginning of the world: grant this, we beseech Thee, O merciful Father, through Jesus Christ, our Mediator and Redeemer.

Amen.

The grace of the Lord Jesus Christ, and the love of God, and the communion of the Holy Ghost, be with you all.

Amen.

The Order of Service

at the

Ordination of Ministers.

Divine Service shall be celebrated according to the usual order, or to such special order as the Presbytery may judge proper, by one or more Ministers appointed for the purpose.

After the Sermon, the presiding Minister shall read from the pulpit a Narrative, previously approved by the Presbytery, of the proceedings of the Presbytery preparatory to the solemnity in hand, concluding with these words:—

All having accordingly been so far done in this matter as is required by the law and usage of the Church, the Presbytery will now proceed*

---

* When a Minister already ordained is merely to be inducted into a new office, the words will be as follows: "The Presby-

to ordain the said A. B. to the holy ministry [and thereafter to receive and admit him to the office of   ] as soon as he shall have answered satisfactorily the questions appointed by the Church.

Then the Candidate, standing up in the face of the Congregation present, shall answer the questions appointed by the Church to be put to those who are to be ordained to the ministry, or admitted to any charge.

[*These questions, according to Act* 10, *Assembly* 1711, *are as follows :—*]

1. Do you believe the Scriptures of the Old and New Testaments to be the Word of God, and the only rule of faith and manners ? *Answer*—I do.

2. Do you sincerely own and believe the whole doctrine contained in the Confession of Faith, approven by the General Assemblies of this Church, and ratified by law in the year 1690, to be founded upon the Word of God ; and do you acknowledge the same as the confession of your faith ; and will you firmly and constantly adhere thereto, and to the utmost of your power assert, maintain, and defend the

tery will now proceed to receive and admit the said A. B. to the office of   , as soon," &c.

same and the purity of worship as presently practised in this national Church, and asserted in Act 15, Assembly 1707, entitled, Act against innovations in the worship of God? *Answer—* I so believe and promise.

3. Do you disown all Popish, Arian, Socinian, Arminian, Bourignian, and other doctrines, tenets, and opinions whatsoever, contrary to or inconsistent with the foresaid Confession of Faith? *Answer—*I do.

4. Are you persuaded that the Presbyterian government and discipline of this Church are founded upon the Word of God, and agreeable thereto; and do you promise to submit to the said government and discipline, and to concur with the same, and never to endeavour, directly or indirectly, the prejudice or subversion thereof, but to the utmost of your power, in your station, to maintain, support, and defend the said discipline and Presbyterian government by Kirk-sessions, Presbyteries, Provincial Synods, and General Assemblies, during all the days of your life? *Answer—*I so believe and promise.

5. Do you promise to submit yourself willingly and humbly, in the spirit of meekness, unto the admonitions of the brethren of this Presbytery, and to be subject to them and all other Presbyteries, and superior judicatories of

this Church, where God in His providence shall cast your lot: and that according to your power, you shall maintain the unity and peace of this Church against error and schism, notwithstanding of whatever trouble or persecution may arise, and that you shall follow no divisive course from the present established doctrine, worship, discipline, and government of this Church? *Answer*—I do.

6. Are not zeal for the honour of God, love to Jesus Christ, and desire of saving souls, your great motives and chief inducements to enter into the function of the holy ministry, and not worldly designs and interest? *Answer*—I trust so.

7. Have you used any undue methods, either by yourself or others, in procuring this call? *Answer*—I have not.

8. Do you engage, in the strength and grace of Jesus Christ our Lord and Master, to rule well your own family, to live a holy and circumspect life, and faithfully, diligently, and cheerfully to discharge all the parts of the ministerial work, to the edification of the body of Christ? *Answer*—I do, trusting to the help of God.

[9. Do you accept of, and close with, the call to be pastor of this parish, and promise through grace to perform all the duties of a faithful

minister of the Gospel among this people?*
Answer—I do, trusting to the help of God.]

Then may be sung Psalm lxviii. 18-20—

>Thou hast, O Lord, most glorious,
>   Ascended up on high;
>And in triumph victorious led
>   Captive captivity:
>Thou hast received gifts for men,
>   For such as did rebel;
>Yea, ev'n for them, that God the Lord
>   In midst of them might dwell.
>
>Bless'd be the Lord, who is to us
>   Of our salvation God;
>Who daily with His benefits
>   Us plenteously doth load.
>He of salvation is the God,
>   Who is our God most strong;
>And unto God the Lord from death
>   The issues do belong.

The presiding Presbyter shall then descend from the pulpit, and shall pray as follows, the person to be ordained kneeling before him, and the other Presbyters standing around:—

ALMIGHTY God, eternal Fountain of light and life, we Thine unworthy servants whom Thou hast called to minister unto Thee,

---

* This question is to be put only when the person ordained is also to be invested with the office of pastor over the congregation present.

humbly draw near to Thee, through Jesus Christ Thy well-beloved Son, our divine Prophet, Priest, and King, whom in Thine infinite love and wisdom Thou hast given to be the Redeemer of the world, and Head over all things to Thy Church. Vouchsafe to us, O God, for His sake, Thy presence and Thy grace. O be merciful unto us, and bless us, and cause Thy face to shine upon us; that Thy way may be known upon earth; Thy saving health among all nations.

Accept, O God, the sacrifice of thanks and praise which we offer unto Thee. For all Thy love manifested in the great redemption; for all that Christ our Saviour did, and taught, and suffered; for His victory over sin and death; for His triumphant resurrection and ascension; for the gift and indwelling of the Holy Ghost; the comfort of Thy Word and ordinances; the preservation of Thy Church on earth, and the glory prepared for it in heaven; we desire, with angels and just men made perfect, and with Thy whole Church militant upon earth, to magnify and adore Thy name. Glory to God in the highest, and on earth peace, goodwill toward men.

Especially do we at this time bless Thee, that when Jesus Christ Thy Son ascended up on high, He was pleased to call the children of men to be His ministers, and gave gifts unto them, that they might, as apostles and prophets, lay the foundations of His Church, and as evangelists, pastors, and teachers, in perpetual succession, enlarge and feed and guide the same, promising to be with them always, until His second coming in majesty to judge the world.

And now, O God, look down, we earnestly beseech Thee, with favour upon this Thy servant, who is called and offers himself to take part in this great work. Cleanse him from all iniquity; purify and comfort his heart. And as we, in Thy name, do by the imposition of our

[*Here the presiding Presbyter shall lay his hands upon the head of the Candidate, the other Presbyters standing near laying on each his right hand.*]

hands, ordain him a Presbyter in Thy Church, and commit unto him authority to minister Thy Word and Sacraments, O do Thou, who healest what is infirm, and suppliest what is wanting, receive and strengthen him for Thy service, giving him the unction of the Holy Ghost.

Increase in him all needful gifts of Thy grace. Give him a true understanding and a firm belief of Thy holy Word, that knowing himself the power thereof, he may faithfully and effectually make it known to others. Endue him with a burning zeal for Thy glory and for the salvation of men. Sanctify him in body, soul, and spirit. Guide, uphold, and prosper him in all the work of his ministry, to the praise of Thy name, the advancement of Thy kingdom, the comfort of Thy Church, and the discharge of his own conscience in the day of the Lord Jesus; to whom, with thee, O Father, and the Holy Spirit, be all honour and glory, world without end.

Amen.

The person ordained then standing up, the presiding Presbyter, and the others in succession, shall take him by the right hand, saying—

We give you the right hand of fellowship, to take part with us in this ministry.

The presiding Presbyter shall then return to the pulpit, and, if the person ordained is, at the same time, to be instituted, by Act of the Presbytery, to the office of Pastor of a Church, or any other office, shall add these words:—

In the name of the Lord Jesus Christ, and by appointment of this Presbytery, I receive and admit you to the office of .
And may grace, mercy, and peace, from God the Father, Son, and Holy Ghost, be with you always.

Amen.

Thereafter the presiding Presbyter shall give a solemn charge to the new Minister, and (if he is at the same time inducted as a Pastor) to the people present, setting forth their respective duties, from the Word of God.

Then shall be offered the following Prayer, at the Institution of a Pastor :—

ALMIGHTY God, who, under Thine everblessed Son, the great Shepherd of Thy sheep, hast appointed them to be fed and guided by Thy ministering servants; we thank Thee that Thou hast this day graciously provided a Pastor for a portion of Thy flock; and we earnestly entreat Thee to grant unto Thy servant to whom this solemn charge is now committed by us in Thy name, Thy Holy Spirit, to fit him more and more for the work to which he has been called. Give him utterance that he may boldly make known Thy Word and will, and faithfully dispense the mysteries of Thy Gospel. Endue him with wisdom and valour to rule aright the people over whom he is set, and to preserve them in peace and purity, so that Thy Church, under his administration and example, may increase in numbers and in holiness. Grant him meekness, patience, and firmness to bear all the trials and troubles of his ministry, and strengthen him with Thy Spirit, that he may abide steadfast to the end, and be received, with all Thy faithful servants, into the joy of his Lord. Give grace also to those over whom he has been appointed, that they may reverently receive his doctrine and godly admonitions, yielding him all due respect and obedience according to Thy holy Word, and earnestly endeavouring so to profit by his labours, that they may grow in grace, and be made partakers of eternal life, through Jesus Christ our Saviour; to whom, with Thee, O Father, and with the Holy Ghost, be glory, as it was in the beginning, is now, and ever shall be, world without end.

Amen.

When the person ordained is appointed to the office or function of an Evangelist or Missionary, the following Prayer of Institution shall be used instead of that immediately preceding:—

O MOST gracious and merciful God, who hast commanded Thy Gospel to be preached unto all nations, that the ends of the earth may see Thy salvation; we give Thee thanks that, from age to age, Thou dost inspire Thy chosen servants with a desire to make known Thy truth to those who are sitting in darkness, that they may be delivered from sin and death, and made partakers of our hope and joy. And we beseech Thee greatly to bless Thy servant here before

Thee, whom in Thy name we send forth to this good work. O strengthen his hands and encourage his heart for all the special dangers, and difficulties, and temptations that may lie before him. In all his trials may his faith in Thy promises and love abide unshaken, and his hope be constant in Thee. Grant him grace to preach boldly and faithfully the unsearchable riches of Christ, to instruct with meekness those who are opposed to the truth, and to gather into the fold of Christ many who are wandering in the ways of error and of sin. Give him a mouth and wisdom, which all the adversaries he may encounter shall not be able to gainsay or to resist. Grant that going forth in meekness of wisdom, and labouring in entire dependence on Thee, he may reap abundant fruit of his labours in the conversion of souls unto Christ, and obtain the reward of a faithful servant in Thy heavenly kingdom, when they who have turned many unto righteousness shall shine as the stars for ever. These blessings, and all that Thou seest to be for the good of Thy servant and the honour of Thy name, we earnestly implore, through Jesus Christ Thy Son; to whom, with the Father and the Holy Ghost, be all praise and glory, world without end.

Amen.

ORDINATION SERVICE.

When the person ordained is instituted to the office or function of a Teacher or Doctor in a School of Theology, or Seminary of the Church, the Prayer of Institution shall be as follows:—

O GOD, our heavenly Father, who, when we were sunk in darkness and sin, didst send Thy Son to be the Light of the world, and whose Word and Spirit alone can guide us into the way of truth and happiness; send down, we pray Thee, Thy blessing on this Thy servant, now appointed to discharge the office of a teacher in Thy Church, and to make known the mysteries of Thy holy Gospel. Strengthen all his faculties, inspire him with a pure and fervent love of the truth as it is in Jesus, and grant that by earnest study and prayer he may daily grow in the understanding of Thy Word, and become mighty in the knowledge of the Scripture. Give him wisdom, faithfulness, and skill to teach Thy truth, and to uphold it against all false doctrine. And graciously preserve those who shall be committed to his care from all error and delusion, that they be not spoiled through philosophy and vain deceit, after the tradition of men and the rudiments of the world; but grant that, their faith standing not in the wisdom of men, but in the power of God, they may be fitted both to defend and to extend in this dark world the saving knowledge of Jesus Christ Thy Son, in whom are hid all the treasures of knowledge and wisdom, and to whom, with Thee the Father and the Holy Spirit, we ascribe all honour and glory, now and for ever.

Amen.

The Service shall conclude with singing, and the following Benediction:—

Now the God of peace, that brought again from the dead our Lord Jesus Christ, that great Shepherd of the sheep, through the blood of the everlasting covenant, make you perfect in every good work to do His will, working in you that which is well-pleasing in His sight, through Jesus Christ; to whom be glory for ever and ever.

Amen.

NOTE.—*That where a person previously ordained is inducted to a pastoral or other office, the presiding Minister shall, immediately after receiving satisfactory answers to the questions prescribed by the Church, pass on to the words:* In the name of the Lord Jesus Christ, and by appointment of this Presbytery, I receive and admit you to the office, &c. *And shall then proceed to the Charge and Prayer of Institution.*

Appendix.

The following Prayers may be used in the Services of the Church, at the discretion of the Minister.

I.

Confessions.

1.

GIVE ear, O Lord, unto our prayer, and hearken to our supplications; for we acknowledge our iniquities, and lay bare our sins before Thee. Against Thee, O Lord, have we sinned; to Thee do we make our confession, and implore forgiveness. Turn Thy face, O Lord, upon Thy servants, whom Thou hast redeemed with the most precious blood of Thy dear Son. Spare us, we beseech Thee; pardon our offences; and be pleased to extend to us Thy loving-kindness and mercy: through Jesus Christ our Lord.

2.

O Lord, the great and dreadful God, keeping the covenant and mercy to them that love Him, and to them that keep His commandments; we have sinned, and have committed iniquity, and have done wickedly, and have rebelled, even by departing from Thy precepts and from Thy judgments. O Lord, righteousness belongeth unto Thee, but unto us confusion of face, as at this day. To the Lord our God belong mercies and forgivenesses, though we have rebelled against Him: neither have we obeyed the voice of the Lord our God, to walk in His laws which He set before us. O our God, incline Thine ear and hear; open Thine eyes and behold: for we do not present our supplications before Thee for our righteousnesses, but for Thy great mercies. O Lord, hear; O Lord, forgive; O Lord, hearken and do: defer not, for Thine own sake, O our God, for we are called by Thy name.

Prayers for Pardon and Peace.

1.

Almighty and most merciful God, who willest not the souls of sinners to perish, but their faults; restrain the anger which we deserve, and pour out upon us the clemency which we entreat, that through Thy mercy we may pass from mourning into joy: through Jesus Christ our Lord.

2.

O God, who purifiest the hearts of those who confess their sins unto Thee, and absolvest the self-accusing conscience from all bonds of iniquity; give pardon to the guilty, and vouchsafe healing to the wounded, that they may receive remission of all sins, and persevere henceforward in sincere devotion to Thy service : through Jesus Christ our Lord.

3.

O Lord, pour not out Thine anger upon us, neither chasten us in Thy hot displeasure ; but according to Thy mercy show that Thou art the physician of souls : heal our souls, guide us to the haven of Thy will, enlighten our hearts in the knowledge of Thy truth, and grant us to pass the remainder of this day, and of our whole life, in peace, and without sin : for Thine is the dominion, and the power, and the glory, for ever and ever.

II.

Supplications.

1.

MAKE us perfect in Christ Jesus: out of His fulness may we all receive, and rest in Him for evermore.

May His passion be our deliverance; His wounds, our healing; His cross, our redemption; and His death, our life.

With His righteousness may we be clothed; by His Spirit may we be sanctified; in His blood may we be cleansed; and to His image may we be conformed.

May we be in Him as branches in the vine; may He be in us the hope of glory, and unto us all in all.

May He be our Prophet to instruct us, our Priest to intercede for us, and our King to reign over us.

As He died, may we die unto sin; as He rose again, may we rise unto newness of life; suffering with Him here, may we reign with Him hereafter; and bearing now His cross, may we hereafter wear His crown.

2.

Take from us that carnal mind which is death, and increase in us, ever more, and more that spiritual mind which is life and peace.

Give us earnestness, strength of purpose, simplicity of faith, warmth of love.

Make us kindly in thought; gentle in word; generous in deed.

Teach us that it is better to give than to receive; better to forget ourselves than to put ourselves forward; better to minister than to be ministered unto; better to be last than to be first.

Preserve and keep us in the constant sense of our membership of Christ; in the unfailing thought that we are His soldiers and servants; in the love of our Father's house; and in the hope of our eternal home.

May we live by faith in Christ; may we increase in union with Him; may we this day and every day become more and more like Him, till we see Him as He is, and be changed into His perfect likeness.

3.

Take from us all impurity of thought or desire; all envy, pride, hypocrisy; all falsehood and deceit; all covetousness, vainglory, and indolence; all malice and anger: everything that is contrary to Thy will, O most holy Lord.

Enlighten our understandings, that we may know the wonderful things of Thy law, the greatness of Thy love in Christ, the mysteries of Thy kingdom, and the riches of Thine eternal glory.

Teach us what Thou wouldst have us to do; and uphold us by Thy mighty power, that every work of ours may begin always from Thee, and by Thee be happily ended.

Shed abroad Thy love in our hearts, that we may love Thee above all things, and our neighbour as ourselves; and by that charity which never faileth be abundantly refreshed in all our toils and sufferings.

III.

Thanksgivings.

1.

ALMIGHTY God, who, dwelling in the highest heaven, vouchsafest to regard the lowest creature upon earth; we humbly adore, and, with all the powers of our soul, praise Thy holy name for all the blessings Thou hast bestowed upon us. We bless Thee for electing us in Thy favour, creating us in Thine image, redeeming us by Thy Son, and sanctifying us by Thy Spirit; for preserving us amid all the changes and encounters of this life, and raising our thoughts to the hope of a better life to come. May we love Thee as Thou hast loved us; as we have been redeemed by Thy mercy, may we dedicate ourselves to Thy service, that we who have received from Thee things that are holy and blessed, may be ourselves holy and blessed for evermore.

2.

We give thanks unto Thee, O God of our salvation, that Thou hast crowned our lives with mercies; we look unto Thee as the Saviour and benefactor of our souls. Thou hast given us rest during the past night, and hast raised us from our beds in strength, and brought us to the worship of Thine adorable name : wherefore we worship Thee, O God. Bless us, and enable us to sing to Thee as we ought with the understanding, and without ceasing to pray to Thee, working out, with the help of Thy Christ, our salvation with fear and trembling. For Thou art the Prince of Peace, and Saviour of our souls, and to Thee we ascribe all glory.

Thou didst create heaven and earth, and all things that are therein. Thou gavest unto us life and being. By Thy providence are the fruits of the earth preserved to us; and by Thy blessing we, and all things living, are nourished and sustained. Thou openest Thine hand and fillest us with plenty. Thou hast preserved us all our days, and now again Thou bringest us into Thy presence, satisfied with Thy mercies, and replenished with Thy goodness.

Blessed be the Lord, who daily loadeth us with benefits, even the God of our salvation. He that is our God is the God of salvation; and unto God the Lord belong the issues from death.

3.

Glory be to God on high, and on earth peace, goodwill towards men. We praise Thee, we bless Thee, we worship Thee, we glorify Thee, we give thanks to Thee for Thy great glory, O Lord God, heavenly King, God the Father Almighty.

Thou art worthy, O Lord, to receive glory and honour and power, for Thou hast created all things, and for Thy pleasure they are and were created; for Thou didst send Thine only-begotten and well-beloved

Son into the world, that whosoever believeth on Him should not perish, but have everlasting life; for He was slain, and has redeemed men by His blood out of every kindred, and tongue, and people, and nation, and has made them unto Thee kings and priests; and they shall reign on the earth.

We praise Thee, O Lord; we bless Thy name for ever and ever. Every day will we bless Thee, and we will praise Thy name for ever and ever. Not unto us, O Lord, not unto us, but to Thy name be the glory and the praise, for Thy mercy and Thy truth's sake. Henceforth and for evermore we will praise Thy holy name.

4.

Most merciful and gracious God, who hast of Thy great goodness brought us again into Thy presence, we yield unto Thee our unfeigned thanksgiving for all Thine unspeakable benefits. We bless and magnify Thy holy name that Thou hast taught us to know Thee, the only true God, and Jesus Christ whom Thou hast given for us, and made Head over all things unto Thy Church, which is His Body, the fulness of Him that filleth all in all. We joy in Thee through our Lord Jesus Christ, by whom we have received the Atonement; and through whom we have free access into Thy presence, by the Holy Ghost, the blessed Comforter, whom Thou hast given to abide with us and to dwell in us for ever. Blessed be Thy holy name for the unction of the Holy One, in whose light we see light. Thou revealest Thyself unto us as Thou dost not unto the world, that we may comprehend with all saints the exceeding greatness of Thy love, which passeth knowledge, and be filled with all the fulness of God. Wherefore we fall down before Thee; we worship Thee; we glorify Thee; we give thanks unto Thee for Thy great glory, O Lord God, heavenly King, God the Father Almighty.

IV.

Prayers for Illumination.

1.

ALMIGHTY God, with whom are hid all the treasures of wisdom and knowledge, open our eyes, that we may behold wondrous things out of Thy law, and give us grace that we may clearly understand and heartily choose the way of Thy commandments; through Jesus Christ our Lord.

2.

O God, whose inspiration giveth understanding, and who didst bestow upon Thy servants of old, gifts of wisdom, and knowledge, and utterance; be pleased so to guide and direct the hearts and lips of us Thy servants who are here assembled before Thee, that our speaking and hearing may be to our satisfaction and profit; to the increase of our knowledge, and faith, and obedience; and to our comfort and growth in grace: through Jesus Christ our Lord.

V.

Ascriptions of Praise,

With which the Sermon may be ended.

1.

BLESSING, and honour, and glory, and power, be unto Him that sitteth upon the throne, and unto the Lamb for ever and ever.
Amen.

2.

Now unto the King eternal, immortal, invisible, the only wise God, be honour and glory for ever and ever.
Amen.

3.

Now unto Him that is able to do exceeding abundantly above all that we ask or think, according to the power that worketh in us; unto Him be glory in the Church by Christ Jesus, throughout all ages, world without end.
Amen.

4.

Now unto Him that is able to keep us from falling, and to present us faultless before the presence of His glory with exceeding joy; to the only wise God our Saviour, be glory and majesty, dominion and power, both now and ever.
Amen.

5.

Unto Him that loved us, and washed us from our sins in His own blood, and hath made us kings and priests unto God, His Father; to Him be glory and dominion for ever and ever.
Amen.

6.

Now unto the blessed and only Potentate, the King of kings, and Lord of lords; who only hath immortality, dwelling in the light which no man can approach unto; whom no man hath seen or can see: to Him be honour and power everlasting.
Amen.

7.

Now unto the God of all grace, who hath called us unto His eternal glory by Christ Jesus, be glory and dominion for ever and ever.
Amen.

8.

And now to the Father, Son, and Holy Ghost, three Persons, and one God, be ascribed by us, and by the whole Church, as is most due, the kingdom, the power, and the glory, for ever and ever.

Amen.

VI.

Intercessions.

1.

O LORD our heavenly Father, high and mighty, King of kings, Lord of lords, the only Ruler of princes, who dost from Thy throne behold all the dwellers upon earth: most heartily we beseech Thee with Thy favour to behold her most sacred Majesty Queen Victoria, and so replenish her with the grace of Thy Holy Spirit that she may always incline to Thy will, and walk in Thy way; endue her plenteously with heavenly gifts; grant her in health and wealth long to live; strengthen her that she may vanquish and overcome all her enemies; and finally, after this life, she may attain everlasting joy and felicity, through Jesus Christ our Lord.

Almighty God, the fountain of all goodness, we humbly beseech Thee to bless Albert Edward Prince of Wales, the Princess of Wales, and all the Royal Family. Endue them with Thy Holy Spirit; enrich them with Thy heavenly grace; prosper them with all happiness; and bring them to Thine everlasting kingdom, through Jesus Christ our Lord.

[Most gracious God, we humbly beseech Thee, as for this kingdom in general, so especially for the High Court of Parliament at this time assembled, that thou wouldst be pleased to direct and prosper all their consultations to the advancement of Thy glory, the good of Thy Church, the safety, honour, and welfare of our sovereign and her dominions; that all things may be so ordered and settled by their endeavours upon the best and surest foundations, that peace and happiness, truth and justice, religion and piety, may be established among us for all generations.]

We beseech Thee to hear us, good Lord:
That it may please Thee to endue the Lords of the Council and all the nobility with grace, wisdom, and understanding:
That it may please Thee to bless and keep the magistrates, giving them grace to execute justice and to maintain truth:
That it may please Thee to bless and keep all the people:
That it may please Thee to give and preserve to our use the kindly fruits of the earth, so as in due time we may enjoy them:
That it may please Thee to give to all nations unity, peace, and concord.

We beseech Thee to hear us, good Lord:
That it may please Thee to rule and govern Thy holy Church universal in the right way:
That it may please Thee to illuminate all pastors and ministers of Thy Church with true knowledge and understanding of Thy Word, and that both by

their preaching and living they may set it forth and show it accordingly:

That it may please Thee to remove all false doctrine, heresy, and schism:

That it may please Thee to give to all Thy people increase of grace to hear meekly Thy Word, and to receive it with pure affection, and to bring forth the fruits of the Spirit:

That it may please Thee to bring into the way of truth all such as have erred and are deceived:

That it may please Thee to strengthen such as do stand, and to comfort and help the weak-hearted, and to raise up them that do fall, and finally to beat down Satan under our feet.

We beseech Thee to hear us, good Lord:

That it may please Thee to succour, help, and comfort all who are in danger, necessity, and tribulation:

That it may please Thee to preserve all who travel by land or by water, all women labouring of child, all sick persons and young children, and to show Thy pity upon all prisoners and captives:

That it may please Thee to defend and provide for the fatherless children and widows, and all who are desolate and oppressed:

That it may please Thee to have mercy upon all men.

O God, merciful Father, that despisest not the sighing of a contrite heart, nor the desire of such as be sorrowful; mercifully assist our prayers that we make before Thee in all our troubles and adversities whensoever they oppress us; and graciously hear us, that those evils which the craft and subtilty of the devil or man worketh against us be brought to nought, and by the providence of Thy goodness they may be dispersed, that we Thy servants, being hurt by no persecutions, may evermore give thanks unto Thee in Thy holy Church; through Jesus Christ our Lord.

O God, from whom all holy desires, all good counsel, and all just works do proceed, give unto Thy servants that peace which the world cannot give, that our hearts may be set to obey Thy commandments; and also that we, being defended from the fear of our enemies, may by Thy protection pass our time in peace and quietness; through Jesus Christ our Lord.

Amen.

2.

We pray, O Lord, for our beloved country. Take the United Kingdom, with all its colonies and dependencies, under the shadow of Thy wings. Bless and long preserve Thy servant our Sovereign Lady the Queen, the Prince and Princess of Wales, and all the members of the Royal Family; the nobles, judges, and magistrates; the army and navy, and all who are called to the public service. Replenish them with heavenly gifts, that they may faithfully serve Thee, to the end that we, being secured from all enemies, may lead a quiet and peaceable life in all godliness and honesty.

And since it is Thy will that we should pray for all men, we beseech Thee to extend the blessings of

Thy Holy Gospel, that it may be preached everywhere, and everywhere accepted, and all flesh magnify Thy holy name in word and in deed. Give Thy Son the heathen for His inheritance, and the uttermost parts of the earth for His possession; and let the kingdoms of this world become the kingdom of our Lord, and of His Christ. Everywhere break the chains of idolatry and error, and make Thy truth triumphant, that the earth may be glad, and Thy saints shout aloud for joy. Send forth, we beseech Thee, labourers into the fields which are ripe for the harvest, and replenish all Thy ministers with heavenly grace, that they may faithfully serve Thee. We pray for Thy holy Church universal, that all those who profess Thy name may be careful to maintain good works, the weak strengthened, the wanderers restored, the sorrowful comforted, and the doubting confirmed. We beseech Thee to bless this parish and congregation. May its officers and members continually walk in the fear of the Lord, and the comfort of the Holy Ghost. Revive Thy work among us, and pour out abundantly of the spirit of grace and supplication.

We pray for all in sorrow, that they may be speedily relieved and comforted by the Holy Spirit. We would remember them that are in bonds, as bound with them, and them which suffer adversity, as being ourselves also in the body. Let the sighing of the prisoner come before Thee, and save Thou those that are appointed to die. We pray for Christians who suffer for their faith in Thee, that, sustained by Thy love, they may be steadfast in life and in death. We pray for the sick, that they may be restored, if it be Thy holy will, but especially that they may be prepared for every event Thou mayest send. We pray for young children, that their tender life may be precious in Thy sight, and they, through a pious nurture, be fitted for usefulness in this world, and glory in the life to come. We pray for the tempted, that, taking the shield of faith, they may be able to quench all the fiery darts of the wicked; for all who seek salvation, that they may be led to Jesus, the Saviour from sin and death; and for the dying, that Thy rod and Thy staff may comfort them in the dark valley. We pray for the bereaved, that their mourning may be turned into joy, and their souls blessed through the exercise of Thy chastening. We pray for the widow and the fatherless, and for those who have none to help them but Thee, O God. We pray for those who are absent from their homes on the land or on the sea, that they may be kept from danger, and death, and sin. We pray for the stranger in a strange land, and for all who need Thy cheering grace. We pray for the impenitent and ungodly, that they may be convinced of sin, and led to believe in the only name given under heaven whereby we must be saved.

Hear this our prayer; and strengthen us, that we may overcome all temptations, and hereafter receive the crown of life. We ask Thee for all these things in the name of our faithful Lord and Saviour Jesus Christ: to whom, with the Father and the Holy Ghost, be glory for ever and ever.

Amen.

3.

At Evening Prayer.

O Thou whom cherubim and seraphim continually do praise, the heavens and all the powers therein; open Thou our mouths, that we may show forth Thy praise, and declare the greatness of Thy holy name. Grant unto us to have our portion with them who fear Thee in truth, and who obey Thy commandments; for to Thee is due all glory, honour, worship, Father, Son, and Holy Ghost, throughout all ages.

O God Most High, who alone art exalted, having immortality, and dwelling in the light which no man can approach unto; Thou hast made all things by Thy wisdom, separating between the light and the darkness, setting the sun to rule the day, and the moon to rule the night. Thou hast given us grace to come before Thee at this time, to offer unto Thee our evening song of adoration and praise; grant unto us peace for the present evening and coming night; clothe us with the armour of light; and being enlightened by Thy law, give us with joy to persevere in glorifying Thy goodness, offering prayers and supplications to Thy compassion for our fellow-sinners, and for all Thy people: which do Thou grant, according to Thy goodwill towards men.

We remember in Thy presence all for whom we should beseech Thee, that they may receive the dew of Thy blessing, and the outpouring of Thy Holy Spirit. Revive us, O God; revive Thy Church, we pray Thee; have mercy upon all Thy creatures of mankind; gather all who shall be saved into Thy fold; bring in the fulness of the Gentiles; accomplish the number of Thine elect; and unite and carry onward to perfection all Thy saints. Grant unto Thy servants who shall depart in the faith, rest and joy and peace, in the hope of a blessed resurrection; and hasten the appearing and kingdom of our Lord and Saviour Jesus Christ.

These things we ask, O heavenly Father, in patient confidence and joyful hope, being assured that we ask them according to Thy will; that the voice of Thy Church is heard by Thee, that the intercessions of the Holy Ghost are known unto Thee, and that the mediation of Thy well-beloved Son, our Lord and Saviour, doth prevail with Thee.

Wherefore we glorify Thy name, we fall down before Thy throne, we worship and adore Thy glorious majesty; evermore praising Thee, and saying, Salvation be unto our God which sitteth upon the throne, and unto the Lamb for ever. Blessing, and glory, and wisdom, and thanksgiving, and honour, and power, and might, be unto our God for ever and ever.

Amen.

VII.

Thanksgivings for Special Occasions.

In Time of Harvest.

O LORD God Almighty, the fountain of all goodness, by whose word alone all things receive increase and are brought unto perfection, and by whose appointment the fruits of the earth are given for meat unto the children of men; we offer unto Thee our praises and thanksgivings that Thou hast brought us through the circuit of another year, and that, according to Thy promise, seed-time and harvest have not failed. [Thou hast crowned the year with Thy goodness; the earth at Thy commandment hath brought forth abundantly; and our barns are filled with plenty.] We give thanks unto Thy holy name, we rejoice before Thee and praise Thee for Thy goodness to us and to all the creatures of Thy hand; for Thou art the Giver of all good gifts, and unto Thee we render glory and praise, even unto the Father, and unto the Son, and unto the Holy Ghost, now and for evermore, world without end.

Amen.

For Fair Weather.

O Lord God, who hast justly humbled us by Thy late plague of immoderate rain and waters, and in Thy mercy hast relieved and comforted our souls by this seasonable and blessed change of weather; we praise and glorify Thy holy name for this Thy mercy, and will always declare Thy loving-kindness from generation to generation: through Jesus Christ our Lord; who liveth and reigneth with Thee, O Father, in the unity of the Holy Ghost, one God, world without end.
Amen.

For Rain.

O God, our heavenly Father, who by Thy gracious providence dost cause the former and the latter rain to descend upon the earth, that it may bring forth fruit for the use of man; we give Thee humble thanks that it hath pleased Thee, in our great necessity, to send at the last a joyful rain upon our land, and to refresh it when it was dry, to the great comfort of us Thine unworthy servants, and to the glory of Thy holy name: through Thy mercies in Jesus Christ our Lord, who liveth and reigneth with Thee, O Father, in the unity of the Holy Ghost, one God, world without end.
Amen.

For Deliverance from Dearth.

We yield Thee abounding thanks, O most bountiful God and Father, who hast had compassion upon the multitudes that were ready to perish with hunger; and even as Thou didst make the few loaves and fishes enough for thousands, art now crowning the seed-time with harvest, and filling the land with plenty. And we beseech Thee, that unto this Thy miracle of earthly providence, Thou wilt add Thy richer miracle of heavenly grace, and evermore give us that bread which cometh down from heaven, whereof they that eat shall be nourished unto life eternal; through Jesus Christ our Lord.

Amen.

For Deliverance from Pestilence.

O Lord God of our salvation, who turnest man to destruction, and sayest, Return, ye children of men; we yield Thee hearty thanks for that Thou didst not shut the ears of Thy mercy when we cried unto Thee, in the day of Thy terrible visitation, as out of the valley and shadow of death; but hast mercifully driven from our borders the wasting pestilence, and restored the voice of joy and health into our dwellings. Of Thy mercy it is, O Lord, that we were not utterly consumed and wasted away; and therefore, as the living from the dead, we return to bless, and praise, and magnify Thee; through Jesus Christ our Lord.

Amen.

For Deliverance from War, or other Public Calamity.

O Almighty God, who hast in all ages showed forth Thy power and mercy in all the deliverances of Thy Church, and in the protection of righteous States and nations, maintaining Thy holy and eternal truth; we adore the wisdom and goodness of Thy providence, which hath so timely interposed in our extreme danger, and again filled our hearts with joy and gladness, after that Thou hadst afflicted us. We beseech Thee, give us such a lively and lasting sense of this Thy great mercy towards us, that we may not grow secure, and careless in our obedience, by presuming upon Thy goodness; but that it may lead us to repentance, and move us to be the more zealous in all the duties of our religion, as well to Thee as to one another. Let truth and justice, liberty and order, holiness and piety, concord and unity, with all other virtues, so flourish among us, that they may be the stability of our times, and make this nation a bulwark of Thy Church, and a joy and praise in the earth. So will we, Thy people, and the sheep of Thy pasture, give Thee thanks for ever, and always be showing forth Thy praise from generation to generation: through Jesus Christ our only Saviour and Redeemer, to whom with Thee, O Father, and the Holy Ghost, be glory in the Church throughout all ages, world without end.

Amen.

For Restoring Public Peace at Home.

O eternal God, our heavenly Father, who alone makest men to be of one mind, and stillest the outrage of a violent and unruly people; we bless Thy holy name, that it hath pleased Thee to appease the seditious tumults which have been lately raised up amongst us; most humbly beseeching Thee to grant to all of us grace, that we may henceforth obediently walk in Thy holy commandments; and, leading a quiet and peaceable life in all godliness and honesty, may continually offer unto Thee our sacrifice of praise and thanksgiving for these Thy mercies towards us: through Jesus Christ our Lord, who liveth and reigneth with Thee, O Father, in the unity of the Holy Ghost, one God, world without end.
Amen.

VIII.

Intercessions for Special Occasions.

In Time of Dearth.

O GOD, heavenly Father, whose gift it is that the rain doth fall and the earth bring forth her increase, behold, we beseech Thee, the afflictions of Thy people. Visit the earth with Thy heavenly benediction; and grant that the scarcity and dearth which we now suffer, may, through Thy goodness, be mercifully turned into plenty; that we, receiving Thy bountiful liberality, may use the same to Thy glory, the relief of those that are needy, and our own comfort, for the love of Jesus Christ our Lord; to whom, with Thee and the Holy Ghost, be all honour and glory, now and for ever. Amen.

In Time of a Rainy Harvest.

O God, our Sun and Shield, who hast spared us to see another season of ingathering, renew Thy mercy unto us, we beseech Thee, and stay the falling of the rain from heaven, that the increase which Thou hast given may not be destroyed. We confess that we have been worldly and thankless, and have forgotten that Thou, who crownest the year with Thy goodness, canst turn a fruitful land into barrenness for the wickedness of them that dwell therein. Hear our cry, O Lord, and have mercy upon us, that the field may be joyful, and all that are therein. The waters fly at Thy rebuke: the stormy wind fulfilleth Thy word. Let not the labour of the husbandman be in vain, O our Father: let not the bread of Thy children fail. But do Thou keep from all harm the fruits of the earth, till they be stored in our garners safely and in abundance. And this we ask for the sake of Him who fed the bodies of men with the bread that perisheth, and their souls with the living bread which came down from heaven.

Amen.

In Time of Pestilence.

Holy Lord God Almighty, who of old didst stay the angel of pestilence at the cry of Thy repenting children, and bring back health to a dying people; hear us, Thy suppliants, returning unto Thee, as in sackcloth, dust, and ashes, and mercifully lift from us the heavy hand of Thy righteous visitation, that the people may live before Thee, and not die, and that the land may no longer mourn by reason of Thy judgments, O Lord, who for our iniquities art justly displeased. We humbly ask it for Christ's sake.

Amen.

In Time of War.

O Lord God of infinite mercy, we humbly beseech Thee to look down in compassion upon this kingdom and nation now involved in war. Reckon not against us our many iniquities; pardon our offences, our pride and arrogance, our self-sufficiency and forgetfulness of Thee.

Save and defend our gracious Queen. Give wisdom to her counsellors, skill to her officers, courage and endurance to her soldiers and sailors. Look in mercy on those immediately exposed to peril, conflict, sickness, and death. Comfort the prisoners, relieve the sufferings of the wounded, and show mercy to the dying.

Finally, we beseech Thee to remove, in Thy good providence, all causes and occasions of war; to dispose our hearts and the hearts of our enemies to moderation; and of Thy great goodness to restore peace among the nations: through Jesus Christ our Lord.

Amen.

In Time of Storm or Tempest.

[*Especially in Maritime Places, or at Sea.*]

O most mighty and eternal God, who commandest the winds and seas, and they do obey Thy voice; in dread of Thy great power, yet trusting to Thy mercy, we cry unto Thee, in behalf of all those exposed to peril [*or*, in this our peril and trouble], through this prevailing storm and tempest. We beseech Thee to have mercy upon us, and spare Thy creatures whom Thou hast made. Forgive Thy people who have sinned against Thee; and assuage, we beseech Thee, this storm. Do Thou bid the winds to cease, and let there be a calm. Of Thy great goodness rescue and deliver those who are travelling by land or by water, and especially those [*or*, especially us Thine unworthy servants, whom Thou seest to be] in peril of shipwreck; and grant that, being taught by Thy power, and persuaded by Thy mercy, they, and we, and all Thy people, may henceforth serve Thee in pureness of living and truth, to the glory of Thy holy name: through Jesus Christ our Lord.

Amen.

For a Sick Person desiring the Prayers of the Church.

Almighty God, our heavenly Father, of Thine infinite goodness grant unto the soul of Thy servant, who desires to be remembered in our prayers, the anointing of the Holy Ghost, who is the spirit of all strength, comfort, relief, and gladness. Vouchsafe for Thy great mercy, if it be Thy blessed will, to restore unto *him* bodily health and strength to serve Thee; and send *him* release of all *his* pains, troubles, and diseases, both in body and mind; and howsoever Thy goodness, by Thy divine and unsearchable providence, may dispose of *him*, we, Thine unworthy servants, humbly beseech Thee to do with *him* according to the multitude of Thine innumerable mercies, and to pardon all *his* sins and offences. Vouchsafe, also, mercifully to grant unto *him* strength, by

Thy Holy Spirit, to withstand and overcome all temptations and assaults of the adversary, that in no wise he prevail against *him*, but that *he* may have perfect victory and triumph against the devil, sin, and death: through Christ our Lord, who by His death hath overcome him that had the power of death, and with the Father and the Holy Ghost evermore liveth and reigneth, world without end.
Amen.

For a Sick Child.

O Almighty God and merciful Father, to whom alone belong the issues of life and death, look down from heaven, we humbly beseech Thee, with the eyes of mercy upon this child, now lying upon the bed of sickness. Visit *him*, O Lord, with Thy salvation; deliver *him* in Thy good appointed time from *his* bodily pain, and save *his* soul for Thy mercy's sake; that if it shall be Thy pleasure to prolong *his* days here on earth, *he* may live to Thee, and be an instrument of Thy glory by serving Thee faithfully and doing good in *his* generation; or else receive *him* unto those heavenly habitations, where the souls of those who sleep in the Lord Jesus enjoy perpetual rest and felicity. Grant this, O Lord, for Thy mercy's sake, in the name of Thy Son our Lord Jesus Christ, who liveth and reigneth with Thee and the Holy Ghost, ever one God, world without end.
Amen.

For a Departing Soul.

Almighty God, with whom do live the spirits of just men made perfect, we humbly commend our departing *brother* into Thy hands, as into the hands of a faithful Creator and most merciful Saviour; beseeching Thee that *his* soul may be precious in Thy sight. Wash *him*, we pray Thee, in the blood of that immaculate Lamb that was slain to take away the sins of the world; that whatsoever defilements *he* may have contracted in the midst of this miserable and wicked world, through the lusts of the flesh or the wiles of Satan, being purged and done away, *he* may be presented pure and without spot before Thee. Vouchsafe to *him* a quiet passage, and guide *him* through the valley of the shadow of death. Place *him* in the habitations of light and peace, in the company of Thy saints and faithful people who are gone before: and in the resurrection of the just do Thou make *him* partaker of the heavenly inheritance, there to reign with Thy holy apostles, with the goodly company of prophets and martyrs, and with all Thy saints in glory and blessedness, for ever and ever.
Amen.

For Missions and Missionaries.

1.

O God, who hast made of one blood all nations of men to dwell on all the face of the earth, and didst send Thy blessed Son to preach peace to them that are afar off, and to them that are nigh; grant that all the people of heathen lands may seek after Thee and find Thee: and hasten, O Lord, the fulfilment of Thy promise to pour out Thy Spirit upon all flesh; through Jesus Christ our Lord.

Amen.

2.

O God of Abraham, of Isaac, and of Jacob, have mercy, we beseech Thee, upon Thine ancient people the house of Israel; deliver them from their hardness of heart and unbelief of Thy Gospel; that, their hearts being turned to Thee, they may behold Thy glory in the face of Jesus Christ, and may acknowledge Him to be their Saviour, whom their fathers gave up to be crucified, so that they may be brought into Thy holy Church, and saved among the remnant of the true Israel.

Amen.

3.

Gather together Thine elect, O God our Saviour, from the four corners of heaven; send forth Thy ministers into all the world in the spirit and power of Elias, and bring in the fulness of the Gentiles. Quicken the dead in trespasses and sins, enlighten the ignorant, and bring back the wandering; and, as Thou hast warned us that the day of the Lord so cometh as a thief in the night, grant us grace to be sober, and to watch unto prayer, lest that day come upon us unawares; and evermore to live with our loins girded, as men who wait for their Lord.

Amen.

4.

O most merciful Saviour and Redeemer, who wouldst not that any should perish, but that all men should be saved and come to the knowledge of the truth; fulfil Thy gracious promise to be present with those who are gone forth in Thy name to preach the Gospel of salvation in distant lands. Be with them in all perils by land or by water, in sickness and distress, in weariness and painfulness, in disappointment and persecution. Bless them, we beseech Thee, with Thy continual favour; and send Thy Holy Spirit to guide them into all truth. O Lord, let Thy ministers be clothed with righteousness, and grant that Thy word spoken by their mouths may never be spoken in vain. Endue them with power from on high; and so prosper Thy work in their hands, that the fulness of the Gentiles may be gathered in, and all Israel be saved. Hear us, O Lord, for Thy mercy's sake; and grant that all who are called by Thy name may be one in Thee, and may abound more and more in prayers and in freewill offerings, for the extension of Thy kingdom throughout the world, to Thy honour and glory, who livest and reignest with the Father and the Holy Ghost, ever one God, world without end.

Amen.

5.

Almighty God, who by Thy Son Jesus Christ didst give commandment to the holy apostles that they should go into all the world and preach the Gospel to every creature; grant to us whom Thou hast called into Thy Church a ready will to obey Thy Word, and fill us with a hearty desire to make Thy way known upon earth, Thy saving health among all nations. Look with compassion upon the heathen that have not known Thee, and on the multitudes that are scattered abroad as sheep having no shepherd. O heavenly Father, Lord of the harvest, have respect, we beseech Thee, to our prayers, and send forth labourers into Thine harvest. Fit and prepare them by Thy grace for the work of their ministry: give them the spirit of power, and of love, and of a sound mind; strengthen them to endure hardness; and grant that by their life and doctrine they may show forth Thy glory, and set forward the salvation of all men, through Jesus Christ our Lord.

Amen.

For our Fellow-Countrymen in Heathen Lands.

O Lord, who hast commanded us by Thine apostles to walk worthy of the vocation wherewith we are called, and as we have each received Thy gift, so to minister the same one to another; grant to all who are baptized into Thy holy name, and especially to our fellow-countrymen who sojourn in distant lands, that they may show forth Thy praises, who hast called them out of darkness into marvellous light. Preserve

them, we beseech Thee, from the sin of offending Thy little ones who believe in Thee, and from causing Thy Word to be blasphemed among the heathen. Make them as the salt of the earth, and as a light in the world; that so, beholding their good works, and won by their holy life, multitudes may be turned to Thy truth, to glorify Thee in the day of visitation, who art our Saviour and our God, blessed for ever.
Amen.

For the Young.

O gracious Saviour, who lovest little children, and didst take them into Thy holy arms and bless them: bless now, we pray Thee, the children in this parish. May they grow up in Thy fear and love. May they live ever as members of Christ, children of God, and heirs of heaven. May they give their hearts to Thee, and remember their Creator in the days of their youth; that so they may be Thine for ever, and at length enter the heavenly inheritance which Thou hast purchased for them, who livest and reignest with the Father and the Holy Spirit, one God evermore.
Amen.

Before Election of Elders or Deacons.

Almighty God, the Giver of all good gifts, who by Thy Son Jesus Christ hast appointed diverse administrations for the edifying of His Body in truth, holiness, and charity, mercifully look upon Thy people whom Thou hast redeemed, and at this time so guide and govern them that they may faithfully and wisely make choice of fit *persons* to serve before Thee in Thy Church. And to *those* who shall be appointed to any holy function, give Thy grace and heavenly benediction, that both by *their* life and doctrine *they* may show forth Thy praises, and set forward the salvation of all men, to the glory of Thy great name, and the benefit of Thy holy Church, through Jesus Christ our Lord.

Amen.

For the General Assembly during their Session.

O almighty and everlasting God, who by Thy Holy Spirit didst preside in the first Assembly of the apostles and elders at Jerusalem, and dost still inhabit the whole company of the faithful; mercifully regard, we beseech Thee, Thy servants chosen and gathered before Thee at this time, as a chief court and council of Thy Church. Shed down upon them all heavenly wisdom and grace; enlighten them with true knowledge of Thy Word; inflame them with a pure zeal for Thy glory; and so order all their doings through Thy good Spirit that unity and peace shall prevail among them; that truth and righteousness shall flow forth from them; and that, by their endeavours, all Thy Ministers and Churches shall be established and comforted, Thy Gospel everywhere purely preached and truly followed, Thy kingdom among men extended and strengthened, and the whole body of Thine elect people grow up into Him who is Head over all things to the Church, Jesus Christ our Lord.

Amen.

IX.

Collects and Prayers for Special Occasions.

For the Season of Holy Communion.

1.

O GOD, Father of our Lord Jesus Christ, who dost, in Thy good providence call us to draw near to Thee in Holy Communion, look graciously, we beseech Thee, upon Thy servants who are about to seek Thy grace in this most sacred ordinance. Give unto them true and hearty sorrow for past sins, power to confess the same unto Thee, grace to seek Thy mercy and forgiveness, and an earnest desire to walk before Thee in newness and holiness of life; and mercifully grant that we, with all those who shall come to Thy Holy Table, may be filled with Thy Spirit in the inner man; that drawing near with penitent hearts and lively faith, we may receive the Holy Sacrament to our present and everlasting comfort: through Thy Son our Saviour Jesus Christ.

Amen.

2.

O God, who art the fountain of all holiness, we beseech Thee for the help of Thy continual grace; that, partaking of this Thy Holy Table, as strangers and pilgrims here on earth, we may be advanced to partake of the heavenly feast in the general assembly of all Thy saints in the day of Thy kingdom: through Jesus Christ our Lord, who liveth and reigneth with Thee, O Father, in the unity of the Holy Ghost, one God, world without end.
Amen.

3.

O Lord Jesus Christ, who in Thy last supper with Thy disciples didst ordain in the blessed Sacrament a perpetual memorial of Thy passion until Thy coming again; grant unto us, we beseech Thee, such discernment of Thy holy mysteries, that we may continually receive the full fruition of Thy redeeming love; who livest and reignest with the Father and the Holy Ghost, one God, world without end.
Amen.

The Incarnation of our Lord.

1.

Most merciful God, who hast so loved the world as to give Thine only-begotten Son, that whosoever believeth in Him should not perish but have everlasting life; vouchsafe unto us, we humbly pray Thee,

the precious gift of faith, whereby we may know that the Son of God is come; and, being always rooted and grounded in the mystery of the Word made flesh, may have power to overcome the world, and gain the blessed immortality of heaven; through the merits of this same incarnate Christ, who liveth and reigneth with Thee in the unity of the Holy Ghost, ever one God, world without end.
Amen.

2.

O Almighty God, who by the birth of Thy Holy One into the world didst give Thy true light to dawn upon our darkness; grant that as Thou hast given us to believe in the mystery of His incarnation, and hast made us partakers of the divine nature, so in the world to come we may ever abide with Him, in the glory of His kingdom; through the same Jesus Christ our Lord.
Amen.

The Passion and Crucifixion of our Lord.

1.

O most merciful Father, who of Thy tender compassion towards us guilty sinners didst give Thine only-begotten Son to be an offering for our sins, grant us grace, we humbly beseech Thee, that, being united unto Him by Thy Spirit, and made partakers of His sufferings and His death, we may crucify the corrupt inclinations of the flesh, die daily unto the world, and lead holy and unblameable lives. Cleaving unto His Cross in all the temptations of life, may we hold fast the profession of our faith without wavering, and finally attain unto the resurrection of the just; through the merits of this same once crucified, but now risen and exalted, Saviour.

Amen.

2.

Lord Jesus Christ, Thou holy and spotless Lamb of God, who didst take upon Thyself the curse of sin which was due to us, with all the heavenly host of the redeemed; we unite in ascribing unto Thee power, and riches, and wisdom, and strength, and honour, and glory, and blessing. We bless Thee for all the burdens Thou hast borne, for all the tears Thou hast wept, for all the pains Thou hast suffered, for every drop of blood Thou hast shed, for every word of comfort Thou hast spoken on the cross, for every conflict with the powers of darkness, and for Thine eternal victory over the terrors of death and the pains of hell.

Amen.

The Burial of our Lord.

1.

O Almighty God, who by the descent of our Saviour Jesus Christ into hell, and His rising again from the dead, hast given assurance that the spirits of those who sleep in Him do abide in joy and felicity; grant unto us, we beseech Thee, such steadfast faith and lively hope, that we may purify ourselves as He is pure; and that we, with Thy whole redeemed Church, may speedily attain unto the resurrection from the dead, when our mortal bodies shall put on immortality and incorruption, and we shall be changed into the likeness of His glorious body; who liveth and abideth with Thee and the Holy Ghost, one God, world without end. **Amen.**

2.

Grant, O Lord, that as we are baptized into the death of Thy blessed Son our Saviour Jesus Christ, so by continual mortifying our corrupt affections, we may be buried with Him; and that through the grave and gate of death, we may pass to our joyful resurrection, for His merits, who died and was buried, and rose again for us, Thy Son Jesus Christ our Lord. **Amen.**

The Resurrection of our Lord.

1.

Almighty God, who through Thine only-begotten Son Jesus Christ hast overcome death, and opened unto us the gates of everlasting life; we humbly beseech Thee, that as, by Thy special grace preventing us, Thou dost put into our minds good desires, so by Thy continual help we may bring the same to good effect; through Jesus Christ our Lord, who liveth and reigneth with Thee and the Holy Ghost, ever one God, world without end.

Amen.

2.

Almighty God, who hast brought again from the dead our Lord Jesus, the glorious Prince of salvation, with everlasting victory over hell and the grave; grant unto us power, we beseech Thee, to rise with Him to newness of life, that we may overcome the world with the victory of faith, and have part at last in the resurrection of the just; through the merits of the same risen Saviour, who liveth and reigneth with Thee and the Holy Ghost, ever one God, world without end.

Amen.

3.

O Thou God and Father of our Lord Jesus Christ, we render Thee most humble and hearty thanks that when He had descended into the grave, Thou didst not suffer Thy Holy One to see corruption, but didst show unto Him the path of life and raise Him from the dead, and set Him at Thine own right hand in the heavenly places. Grant us grace, we beseech Thee, to apprehend with true faith the glorious mystery of our Saviour's resurrection, and fill our hearts with joy, and a lively hope that amid all the sorrow, trials, and temptations of our mortal state, and in the hour of death, we may derive strength and comfort from this sure pledge of an inheritance incorruptible and undefiled, and that fadeth not away.

Amen.

The Ascension of our Lord.

1.

O Lord Jesus Christ, Thou Conqueror of death and hell, who from the depths of Thy humiliation didst pass into the heavens, and art crowned with glory and honour as King of saints and eternal High Priest over the house of God; let Thy all-powerful intercessions prevail on our behalf, that, being delivered from the curse of sin, we may receive grace and strength to follow Thee with patient endurance through the sorrows and pains of earth, and the darkness of the grave, and having thus shared in Thy sufferings here, become partakers also of Thy joy and glory in the everlasting kingdom of the Father.

Amen.

2.

O God, the King of glory, who hast exalted Thine only Son Jesus Christ with great triumph into Thy kingdom in heaven; we beseech Thee, leave us not comfortless; but send to us Thy Holy Ghost to comfort us, and exalt us unto the same place whither our

Saviour Christ has gone before, who liveth and reigneth with Thee and the Holy Ghost, one God, world without end.
Amen.

The Descent of the Holy Ghost.

1.

Most glorious and blessed God, who through the Holy Ghost hast made Thy one Catholic Church to be the Body of Christ, the fulness of Him that filleth all in all; we humbly beseech Thee to grant unto us, and to all Thy people, such strong and steadfast faith in this great mystery of grace, that, being safely defended from all heresy and schism, we may ever abide in the unity of the Spirit, and so grow up into Him in all things, which is the Head, even Christ: to whom, with Thee and the Holy Ghost, ever one God, be all honour and praise, world without end.
Amen.

2.

O Almighty God, who hast sent down the Holy Ghost upon Thine elect, endowing them with His manifold gifts, and knitting them together in one communion and fellowship in the mystical Body of Thy Son; grant unto us grace to use all those Thy gifts alway to Thine honour and glory, and to abound in faith, hope, and charity, waiting for Thy Son from heaven: that, when He shall appear, we with all Thy saints may be found of Him in peace, and by Him may be presented before Thy glorious presence with exceeding joy; through the same Jesus Christ our Lord, who liveth and reigneth with Thee, O Father, in the unity of the same Holy Ghost, ever one God, world without end.

Amen.

3.

O Holy Ghost, Spirit of the Father and the Son, who by Thy quickening energy hast raised us up to a new life in Christ Jesus, and dost in mercy to our infirmities condescend to dwell in our mortal bodies as Thy consecrated temples; bring forth in our hearts and lives, we beseech Thee, the fruits of love, joy, peace, long-suffering, gentleness, faith, meekness, and temperance; that so walking in Thee with all holy obedience, we may stand firm in the knowledge and love of the truth, against the wiles of the devil, may overcome the world, and be glorified in the fellowship of the Father and the Son; to whom, with Thee, who art coequal and coeternal God, we ascribe all honour, thanksgiving, and praise.

Amen.

The Advent of our Lord.

1.

Almighty God, we beseech Thee grant unto Thy people grace that they may wait with vigilance for the advent of Thy Son our Lord, that when He shall

arise from Thy right hand to visit the earth in righteousness and Thy people with salvation, He may not find us sleeping in sin, but diligent in Thy service, and rejoicing in Thy praises, that so we may enter in with Him unto the marriage of the Lamb; through His merits, who liveth and reigneth with Thee and the Holy Ghost, ever one God, world without end.
Amen.

2.

God of all grace and comfort, who hast not appointed us unto wrath, but to obtain salvation by our Lord Jesus Christ; aid us, we beseech Thee, at this time, to repent heartily and truly of all our sins, and so to humble ourselves that when He cometh we may be prepared to receive Him with childlike faith, and join in the glad cry, Hosanna to the Son of David! Blessed is He that cometh in the name of the Lord!
Amen.

3.

Almighty God, give us grace that we may cast away the works of darkness, and put upon us the armour of light, now in the time of this mortal life, in which Thy Son Jesus Christ came to visit us in great humility, that in the last day, when He shall come again in His glorious majesty to judge both the quick and dead, we may rise to the life immortal; through Him who liveth and reigneth with Thee and the Holy Ghost, now and ever.
Amen.

4.

O Almighty God, grant that those necessary works wherein we are engaged, whether in the affairs of Thy Church or of this world, may not prevail to hinder us; but that, at the appearing and advent of Thy Son, we may hasten with joy to meet Him, who liveth and reigneth with Thee and the Holy Ghost, ever one God, world without end.
Amen.

At the opening of a Church.

O Lord our God, there is no God beside Thee. Thou alone art worthy to receive adoration and praise, for Thou art holy, and all nations shall come to worship before Thee, when they learn the joy of Thy salvation. We praise Thee, most merciful Father, for the foundation of Thy Church on earth; for Thy sacred oracles, for the ministry of Thy Word, and for Thy holy Sacraments. We give Thee thanks, that by Thy providence this house has been erected for the worship of Thy name. Accept, we beseech Thee, the work of our hands. Let this house be the House of God. Here let Thy presence dwell and Thy glory be revealed. When Thy holy Word is read and preached in this place, and the holy Sacraments are administered, send down upon the congregation the dews of Thy heavenly grace. When Thy people bring to Thee their thanksgiving for the gifts of Thy providence, accept their offering and bless them, that their joy may be full. And when in seasons of calamity and distress they humble themselves before Thee and implore Thy mercy, hear Thou in heaven and pity them; forgive their sins wherein they have transgressed against Thee and deliver them, or else comfort and support them under their trials; and sanctify unto them their affliction, that it may bring forth in them the fruits of salvation and peace. Hear us, we beseech Thee, O God of all grace, Father of all light, and Fountain of all good. Let our prayer come up before Thee and be acceptable through the merits of Jesus Christ, and do unto us according to Thy great mercy and love. And unto Thee, King eternal, immortal, and invisible, who alone art mighty, wise, and good, who dwellest in light which no man can approach unto and live— unto Thee be all glory through Jesus Christ, in heaven and in earth, for ever and ever.

Amen.

On the Laying of the Foundation-Stone of a Church.

Blessed be Thy name, O Lord, that it hath pleased Thee to put it into the hearts of Thy servants to begin the erection of a house in which Thy name is to be worshipped, the glad tidings of salvation proclaimed, and Thy holy Sacraments administered.

Prosper Thou us, O Lord, in this our undertaking. Keep and preserve by Thy providence unto the end the work which is now begun in Thy fear. Excite the skill and animate the industry of the workmen. Shield them from all accidents and dangers. And grant unto them, and all of us here present, the influences of Thy Divine Spirit, so that we may become in soul and body living temples of the Holy Ghost, and be prepared for that eternal city which hath foundations, whose builder and maker is God. All which we ask through the abundant merits of our Lord and Saviour Jesus Christ, who liveth and reigneth with Thee and the Holy Ghost, ever one God, world without end.

Amen.

To be used at Sea.

O eternal Lord God, who alone spreadest out the heavens and rulest the raging of the sea, and hast compressed the waters with bounds, until day and night shall come to an end, be pleased to receive into Thine almighty and most gracious protection the persons of us Thy servants, and the ship [or fleet] in which we serve. Preserve us from dangers of the deep, and from the violence of enemies [that we may be a safeguard unto our country, and a security for such as do business in the mighty waters], that in due season we may return to our homes with a thankful remembrance of Thy mercies; and that, finally, having passed the sea of this troubled life, we may enter the haven of eternal rest; through Him who is our only refuge and Saviour, Jesus Christ our Lord.

Amen.

Almsgiving.

O Lord our Governor, who art King of all the earth; accept, of Thine infinite goodness, the offerings of Thy people, which, in obedience to Thy commandment, in honour of Thy name, and with a free will and joyful heart, we yield and dedicate to Thee: and grant unto us Thy blessing, that the same being devoted to Thy service, may be used for Thy glory, and for the welfare of Thy Church and people; through Jesus Christ our Lord.

Amen.

For those who minister in Holy Things.

O Thou great Shepherd and Bishop of our souls, give unto Thy servants, the ministers of the mysteries of our most holy faith, the spirit of prudence and activity, faith and charity, confidence and zeal, diligence and watchfulness, that they may declare Thy will unto Thy people faithfully, and minister Thy Sacraments rightly. Grant, O Lord, that by a holy life and a true belief, by well-doing, and patient suffering when Thou dost call them to it, they may glorify Thee, the great lover of souls, and, after a plentiful conversion of sinners from the error of their ways, may shine as the stars in glory.

Amen.

For Unity.

1.

O Almighty God, who didst call out Thy holy Church to be one holy body, filled with Thy divine presence and life, and instructed in Thine eternal truth, have mercy upon all who profess and call themselves Christians; lead them, we beseech Thee, out of all their wandering and divisions, and heal all mutual hatred, variance, and animosities, that they may all once more be one in Jesus Christ, as He is one with Thee. Deliver all those who are deceived by the wiles of the enemy and have forsaken the congregation of Thy Church, or been carried away by the vanity of error, and restore them to Thy mercy, to the unity of the truth in the one fold of Jesus Christ, Thy holy Church.

Amen.

2.

O God, the Father of our Lord Jesus Christ, our only Saviour, the Prince of Peace; give us grace seriously to lay to heart the great dangers we are in by our unhappy divisions. Take away all hatred and prejudice, and whatsoever else may hinder us from godly union and concord; that, as there is but one body, and one spirit, and one hope of our calling, one Lord, one faith, one baptism, one God and Father of us all, so we may henceforth be all of one heart, and of one soul, united in one holy bond of truth and peace, of faith and charity, and may with one mind and one mouth glorify Thee; through Jesus Christ our Lord.

Amen.

For Heavenly-Mindedness.

Almighty God, the former of our bodies and Father of our spirits, in whom we live, move, and have our being; shed abroad Thy love in our hearts, we beseech Thee, and cause the comfort of Thy heavenly grace to abound in us, as the earnest and pledge of joys to come; that, casting away all anxious thought for the transitory things of this world, we may seek first Thy kingdom and righteousness, and labour only for that meat which endureth unto everlasting life; through Jesus Christ our Lord.

Amen.

For Guidance.

O God, by whom the meek are guided in judgment, and light riseth up in darkness for the godly: grant us, in all our doubts and uncertainties, the grace to ask what Thou wouldst have us to do; that the Spirit of wisdom may save us from all false choices, and that in Thy light we may see light, and in Thy straight path may not stumble; through Jesus Christ our Lord.

Amen.

For Protection.

O God, who art the author of peace and lover of concord, in knowledge of whom standeth our eternal life, whose service is perfect freedom, defend us Thy humble servants in all assaults of our enemies; that we, surely trusting in Thy defence, may not fear the power of any adversaries; through the might of Jesus Christ our Lord.

Amen.

For Diligence.

1.

O God, who by the example of Thy dear Son hast warned us that we should work Thy works while it is day, before the night cometh, when no man can work; keep us from sloth and idleness, and from the misuse of those talents which Thou hast committed to our trust. Enable us to perform the several duties of our state and calling with such care and diligence that our work may never be reproved in Thy sight; and forasmuch as the needful business of this life is apt to steal away our hearts from Thee, give us grace to remember that we have a master in heaven, and to do everything in singleness of heart, as unto Thee and not unto men, that of Thee we may receive the reward of the inheritance which Thou hast promised in Thy Son our Saviour Jesus Christ.

Amen.

2.

O God, who art the continual defence and protection of all who trust in Thee, and who hast ordained that we should eat bread in the sweat of our brow; we beseech Thee mercifully to prosper the work of our hands, and to sanctify the fruit of our labours to our own good, the good of others, and to Thy glory; and so help us to carry the spirit of Thy holy day into all the business of the week, that whilst our bodies and minds are engaged in honest and useful toil, our hearts may still live and rest in Thee; through Jesus Christ our Lord.

Amen.

3.

O God, who in the beginning didst create the heavens and the earth, and didst give unto all men their work and the bounds of their habitation, grant to us that we be not unwise, but understanding Thy will; not slothful, but diligent in Thy work; that we run not as uncertainly, nor fight Thy battles as those that beat the air; but whatsoever our hand findeth to do, may we do it with our might; that when Thou shalt call Thy labourers to give them their reward, we may so have run that we may obtain, and so have fought the good fight, as to receive the crown of eternal life; through Jesus Christ our Lord.

Amen.

For Humility.

Almighty and everlasting God, the Creator of the ends of the earth, who givest power to the faint, and strength to them that have no might; look mercifully, we beseech Thee, on our low estate, and cause Thy grace to triumph in our weakness, that we may arise and follow in the way of righteousness those who by their faith and patience already inherit the promises; through Jesus Christ our Lord.

Amen.

For Life in Christ.

We approach Thee, O God, in the name of Thy holy child Jesus, who, after He had borne our sins and carried our sorrows upon earth, sat down at Thine own right hand, the Mediator of those for whom He died. Grant us, we beseech Thee, to be made partakers, both in that atonement which He perfected on the cross, and in His mediation in the upper sanctuary, that being reconciled through the death of Thy Son, we may be saved by His life, who liveth and was dead, and is alive for evermore, and hath the keys of hell and of death; to whom be glory, both now and for ever.

Amen.

For Restoration.

O God, who art long-suffering and kind, and art evermore seeking to turn us from our vanities that we may live and not die; grant that we may know this the time of our visitation, and give ear to the voice that calleth us, and so bring us home, good Lord, from wandering in the wilderness, and give our weary hearts such rest in Thee that we may seek to wander from Thee no more, but abide in Thy peace for ever.

Amen.

For Temperance.

Almighty God, gracious Father of men and angels, who openest Thine hand and fillest all things with plenty; teach us to use the gifts of Thy providence soberly and temperately, that our temptations may not be too strong for us, our bodies healthless, or our affections sensual and unholy. Grant, O Lord, that the blessings which Thou givest us may neither minister to sin nor to sickness, but to health and holiness and thanksgiving; that in the strength of Thy provision we may faithfully and diligently serve Thee, may worthily feast at Thy table here, and be accounted worthy to sit down at Thy table hereafter; through Jesus Christ our Lord.

Amen.

For Cheerfulness.

O most loving Father, who willest us to give thanks for all things, to dread nothing but the loss of Thee, and to cast all our cares on Thee who carest for us; preserve us from faithless fears and worldly anxieties, and grant that no clouds of this mortal life may hide from us the light of that love which is immortal, and which Thou hast manifested to us in Thy Son Jesus Christ our Lord.

Amen.

For Faith.

O almighty and everlasting God, who not only givest every good and perfect gift, but also increasest those gifts Thou hast given; we most humbly beseech Thee to increase in us the gift of faith, that we may truly believe in Thee and in Thy promises; and that neither by our negligence, nor infirmity of the

flesh, nor by grievousness of temptation, nor by the subtle crafts and assaults of the devil, we may be driven from faith in our most blessed Lord and Saviour Jesus Christ.
Amen.

For Hope.

O God, by whose wise and righteous order the whole creation groaneth and travaileth in pain together until now, as having been made subject to vanity by reason of sin; graciously help the infirmities of Thy people, we humbly beseech Thee, and raise them up through the strong power of Christian hope; that we also, who have received the first-fruits of the Spirit, may not seek our rest in this mortal state, but inwardly long after that which is far better, to be with Christ in heaven; to whom, with Thee and the Holy Ghost, be honour and glory, world without end.
Amen.

For Love.

Blessed Lord, who hast given us a new commandment that we should love one another, and hast taught us that where envy and strife are, there is confusion and every evil work; give unto us Thy servants grace, that we may be kindly-affectioned one to another, and that there may be no schism among us. Put away from us all bitterness, and wrath, and anger, and evil-speaking, with all malice;

and grant that, in honour preferring one another, we may walk in love, even as Thou, Lord, didst love us, and give Thyself to die for our sins.

Amen.

For Grace.

Almighty and eternal God, who dost bid us walk as pilgrims and strangers in this passing world, seeking that abiding city which Thou hast prepared for us in heaven; we pray Thee so to govern our hearts by Thy Holy Spirit, that we, avoiding all fleshly lusts, which war against the soul, and quietly obedient to the government which Thou hast set over us, may show forth Thy glory before the world by our good works; for Jesus Christ's sake.

Amen.

For Fortitude.

Almighty and most merciful God, whose name is a strong tower into which the righteous runneth and is safe; lift up the standard of Thy Spirit, we beseech Thee, against the power of the enemy, coming in upon us like a flood, and clothe us with the full armour of righteousness on the right hand and on the left, that we may be able to fight manfully the good fight of faith, and so finish our course with joy in the great day when Christ, the righteous Judge, shall appear, who liveth and reigneth with Thee in the unity of the Holy Ghost, ever one God.

Amen.

For Perseverance.

O God, Thou King eternal, immortal, and invisible, the blessed and only Potentate, may we, who cannot see Thee with the eye of flesh, behold Thee steadfastly with the eye of faith, that we faint not under the manifold trials and temptations of this mortal life, but may endure, as seeing Thee who art invisible; that after we have done and suffered Thy will upon the earth, we may enjoy the vision of God in heaven, and may be made partakers of those unspeakable joys, which Thou hast promised to them that love Thee and the appearing of Thy Son Jesus Christ our Lord.
Amen.

For a Blessing on Daily Work.

[*At daily Morning Prayer.*]

1.

O God, who hast commanded that no man should be idle, but that we should all work with our hands the thing that is good; look graciously upon Thy servants now going forth to do their duty, in that station of life unto which Thou hast been pleased to call them. May Thy blessing be upon our persons, upon our labours, upon our substance, and upon all that belongs to us. Enable us to resist the temptations of the world, the flesh, and the devil; to follow the motions of Thy good Spirit, to be serious and holy in our lives; true and just in our dealings;

watchful over our thoughts, words, and actions; diligent in our business, and temperate in all things. Give us grace, that we may honestly improve all the talents Thou hast committed to our trust; and that no worldly business, no worldly pleasures, may ever divert us from the thoughts of the life to come; through Jesus Christ our Lord.

Amen.

2.

Almighty and most merciful Father, who hast given unto us the promise of the life that now is, as well as of that which is to come; we beseech Thee for Thy blessing upon our substance, and that, having food and raiment, we may be therewith content, and may pass our days in peace and quietness.

We pray Thee, therefore, be with Thy servants, who are now going forth unto their work and labour until the evening; and comfort their hearts with a due return for the same.

Bestow Thy grace upon all who are wealthy, that with a free heart they may yield unto the labourer his hire, and be bountiful unto the needy; and do Thou deliver the poor from oppression, and give unto them patience and contentment; for the sake of Jesus Christ our Lord.

Amen.

3.

Direct us, O Lord, in all our doings, with Thy most gracious favour, and further us with Thy continual help; that in all our works begun, continued, and ended in Thee, we may glorify Thy holy name, and finally, by Thy mercy, obtain everlasting life; through Jesus Christ our Lord.

Amen.

The Glorified Saints.

O God, the Father everlasting, whom the glorious hosts of heaven obey, and in whose presence patriarchs, prophets, apostles, martyrs, with all the spirits of the just made perfect, continually do live; fix the eye of our faith, we beseech Thee, with clear and full vision, on the great cloud of witnesses wherewith we are thus compassed about, that laying aside every weight, and the sin that doth so easily beset us, we may run with patience the race that is set before us, and obtain at last the crown of everlasting life; through Jesus Christ our Lord.

Amen.

Communion of Saints.

1.

O Almighty God, who hast built together Thine elect in one communion and fellowship, in the mystical Body of Thy Son Jesus Christ our Lord; grant us grace so to follow Thy blessed saints in all virtuous and godly living, that we may come to those unspeakable and endless joys which Thou hast prepared for them that unfeignedly love Thee; through the same Jesus Christ our Lord.

Amen.

2.

Almighty and everlasting God, the fountain of all life and power, who hast promised to bring up again from the dead the bodies of them who sleep in Jesus; gather not our souls with sinners, we beseech Thee, but make us to be numbered with Thy saints in glory everlasting, that, having been joined with them in one communion here, we may also share hereafter their joyful triumph in the resurrection at the last day; through the same Jesus Christ, our risen and glorified Lord.

Amen.

Remembrance of the Dead.

1.

Blessed Lord, with whom do rest the spirits of Thy departed saints, and who hast said unto us by Thy Spirit, "Blessed are the dead who die in the Lord;" enable us to be followers of them, as they were followers of Christ; and so to run our race with patience, and to fight the good fight of faith, that, our course being finished and our warfare accomplished, we may join the innumerable company of Thy redeemed.

Amen.

2.

O Lord most High, with Thy whole Church throughout the world we give Thee thanks for all

Thy faithful servants who, having witnessed in their lives a good confession, have left the light of their example to shine before Thy people on earth; mercifully grant that by Thy fatherly blessing we may be enabled to follow them in all virtuous and godly living, and that hereafter we may be with them and Thy glorified Son in Thy heavenly presence; through Jesus Christ our Lord.
Amen.

3.

Eternal God, in whom do rest the spirits of just men made perfect; we bless and praise Thy holy name for all Thy servants departed this life in Thy faith and fear: and especially for those most dear to us, of whom we have good hope that they have fallen asleep in Jesus. And we beseech Thee to give us grace to follow their good examples, that even here we may be united to them in fellowship of spirit, and that finally we may be gathered together with them into the bosom of Thy love, through Jesus Christ our Lord.
Amen.

At the Beginning of the Year.

Almighty and eternal God, with whom one day is as a thousand years, and a thousand years as one day, we bring Thee thanks and praise for Thy blessings, more than we can number, with which Thou hast crowned our lives during the year now past; and since Thy mercies are ever new, let the year which has now begun be to us a year of grace and salvation. Have pity upon us in our misery, whose days are as the grass; deliver us from the vanity of our fallen nature, and establish us in the fellowship of that life which is the same yesterday, and to-day, and for ever. Graciously protect and conduct us through the uncertainties of this new year of our earthly pilgrimage; prepare us for its duties and trials, its joys and sorrows; help us to watch and pray, and to be always ready, like men that wait for their Lord; and grant that every change, whether it be of prosperity or adversity, of life or death, may bring us nearer to Thee, and to that great eternal year of joy and rest, which, after the years of this vain earthly life, awaits the faithful in Thy blissful presence; when we shall unite with angels and saints, in ascribing blessing, and honour, and glory, and power, unto Him who sitteth upon the throne, and unto the Lamb for ever and ever.

Amen.

At Morning Prayer.

1.

O Lord our God, holy and incomprehensible, who hast bidden the light to shine out of darkness, who hast refreshed us by nightly slumber, and again wakened us to praise Thy goodness and ask for Thy grace; accept now, in Thine endless mercy, the sacrifice of our worship and thanksgiving, and grant unto us all such requests as may be wholesome for us. Make us to be children of the light and of the day, and heirs of Thine everlasting inheritance; through Jesus Christ our Lord.

Amen.

2.

O God, who dividest the day from the night, separate our deeds from the gloom of darkness; as Thou hast awakened our bodies from sleep, so, we beseech Thee, awaken our souls from sin: as Thou hast caused the light of day to shine on our bodily eyes, cause the light of Thy Word and Holy Spirit to illuminate our hearts; and so give us grace, as the children of light, to walk in all holy obedience before Thy face this day, that in all our thoughts, words, and dealings, we may endeavour to keep faith and a clean conscience towards Thee and towards all men; through Jesus Christ our Lord.

Amen.

3.

O Lord our heavenly Father, almighty and everlasting God, who hast safely brought us to the beginning of this day; defend us in the same with Thy mighty power, and grant that this day we fall into no sin, neither run into any kind of danger, but that all our doings may be ordered by Thy governance to do always that is righteous in Thy sight; through Jesus Christ our Lord.

Amen.

4.

We give Thee thanks, holy Lord, Father Almighty, everlasting God, who hast been pleased to bring us through the night to the hours of morning; we pray Thee to grant us to pass this day without sin, so that at eventide we may again give thanks to Thee; through Jesus Christ our Lord.

Amen.

At Evening Prayer.

1.

Blessed art Thou, O Lord, who hast granted us to pass through this day, and to reach the beginning of the night; hear our prayers, and those of all Thy people; forgive us all our sins, negligences, and ignorances: accept our evening supplications, and send down on Thine inheritance the fulness of Thy mercy and compassion. Compass us about with Thy holy angels, arm us with the armour of Thy righteousness, and guard us by Thy power; deliver us from every assault and device of the adversary, and grant that we may pass this night and all the days of our life in fulness of peace and holiness, without sin or offence; through Jesus Christ our Lord.

Amen.

2.

Almighty and everlasting God, at evening and morning and noonday we humbly beseech Thy divine Majesty that Thou wouldst drive from our hearts the darkness of sin, and make us to come to the true light, which is Christ, our blessed Lord.
Amen.

3.

O Lord God, the life of mortals, the light of the faithful, the strength of those who labour, and the repose of the blessed dead; grant us a peaceful night free from all disturbance, that after an interval of quiet sleep we may by Thy bounty, at the return of light, be endued with activity by Thy Holy Spirit, and enabled in security to render thanks to Thee; through Jesus Christ our Lord.
Amen.

X.

Benedictions.

Wherewith the whole service may be concluded.

1.

THE Lord bless you and keep you: the Lord cause His face to shine upon you, and be gracious unto you: the Lord lift up His countenance upon you, and give you peace.

Amen.

2.

Now the God of peace, that brought again from the dead our Lord Jesus, that great Shepherd of the sheep, through the blood of the everlasting covenant, make you perfect in every good work to do His will, working in you that which is well-pleasing in His sight, through Jesus Christ; to whom be glory for ever and ever.

Amen.

3.

The grace of the Lord Jesus Christ, and the love of God, and the communion of the Holy Ghost, be with you all.
Amen.

4.

The peace of God, which passeth all understanding, keep your hearts and minds in the knowledge and love of God, and of His Son Jesus Christ our Lord; and the blessing of God Almighty, the Father, the Son, and the Holy Ghost, be amongst you, and remain with you always.
Amen.

5.

Grace, mercy, and peace, from God the Father, the Son, and the Holy Ghost, be with you, henceforth and for ever.
Amen.

XI.

Exhortation before the Holy Communion.

(Which may be used instead of that on page 173.)

AS we are now about to celebrate the Holy Communion of the body and blood of Christ, let us consider how St Paul exhorteth all persons to examine themselves before they eat of that bread and drink of that cup. For as the benefit is great, if with a truly penitent heart, and lively faith, we receive that holy Sacrament (for then we spiritually eat the flesh of Christ and drink His blood; then we dwell in Christ and Christ in us, we are one with Christ and Christ with us), so is the danger great if we receive the same unworthily, for then are we guilty of the body and blood of the Lord.

Let us then examine ourselves as to our faith in the doctrines of the Gospel, set forth in the Apostles' Creed, as follows:—

I believe in God the Father Almighty, Maker of heaven and earth; and in Jesus Christ His only Son our Lord, who was conceived by the Holy Ghost, born of the Virgin Mary, suffered under Pontius Pilate, was crucified, dead, and buried: He descended into hell; the third day He rose again from the dead; He ascended into heaven, and sitteth on the right hand of God the Father Almighty; from thence He shall come to judge the quick and the dead. I believe in the Holy Ghost; the holy Catholic Church; the communion of saints; the forgiveness of sins; the resurrection of the body; and the life everlasting.

𝔄men.

But as "faith without works is dead, being alone," let us further examine ourselves whether we truly bear the Christian character, and are living the Christian life.

The Christian character is described by our Lord Himself in the 5th chapter of St Matthew, at the 3d verse, where we read:—

Blessed are the poor in spirit: for theirs is the kingdom of heaven.

Blessed are they that mourn: for they shall be comforted.

Blessed are the meek: for they shall inherit the earth.

Blessed are they which do hunger and thirst after righteousness: for they shall be filled.

Blessed are the merciful: for they shall obtain mercy.

Blessed are the pure in heart: for they shall see God.

Blessed are the peacemakers: for they shall be called the children of God.

Blessed are they which are persecuted for righteousness' sake: for theirs is the kingdom of heaven.

And the Christian life is set forth by St Paul in his Epistle to the Galatians, in the 5th chapter and at the 22d verse:—

But the fruit of the Spirit is love, joy, peace, longsuffering, gentleness, goodness, faith,

Meekness, temperance: against such there is no law.

And they that are Christ's have crucified the flesh with the affections and lusts.

Yet as we must all confess with sorrow that we have not lived thus, let us chiefly now remember the loving-kindness of the Saviour to all such as truly and heartily repented; how He turned not any away from Him; how He blessed the woman which was a sinner, and gave to the penitent thief on the cross the assurance of Paradise.

Let us hear also what comfortable words our Saviour thus saith unto all that truly turn to Him:—

Come unto me, all ye that labour and are heavy laden, and I will give you rest.

Take my yoke upon you, and learn of me; for I am meek and lowly in heart: and ye shall find rest unto your souls.

For my yoke is easy, and my burden is light.

And—

All that the Father giveth me shall come to me; and him that cometh to me, I will in no wise cast out.

Hear also what St Paul saith in his First Epistle to Timothy (1 Tim. i. 15):—

This is a faithful saying, and worthy of all acceptation, that Christ Jesus came into the world to save sinners; of whom I am chief.

Hear also what St John saith (1 John, ii. 1):—

If any man sin, we have an advocate with the Father, Jesus Christ the righteous.

And He is the propitiation for our sins; and not for ours only, but also for the sins of the whole world.

Ye that do truly and earnestly repent you of your sins, and are in love and charity with your neighbours, and purpose to lead a new life, following the commandments of God, and walking from henceforth in His holy ways, draw near with faith and take this holy sacrament to your comfort, considering that the worthiness which the Lord requireth of us is, that we be truly sorry for our sins, and find our joy and salvation in Him. United to Him who is holy, even our Lord Jesus Christ, we are accepted of the Father, and invited to partake of those HOLY THINGS THAT ARE FOR HOLY PERSONS.

THE END.

www.ingramcontent.com/pod-product-compliance
Lightning Source LLC
Chambersburg PA
CBHW022024240426

43667CB00042B/1142